HOW TO R'
PROPERTY

CW009703I7

In this Series

Other titles in preparation

RENT & BUY PROPERTY IN FRANCE

A practical guide for domestic and business users

Clive Kristen

How To Books

British Library Cataloguing-in-publication data
A catalogue record for this book is available from the British Library.

Copyright © Clive Kristen 1993

First published in 1993 by How To Books Ltd, Plymbridge House, Estover Road, Plymouth PL6 7PZ, United Kingdom. Tel: Plymouth (0752) 735251/695745. Fax: (0752) 695699. Telex: 45635.

Note: the material contained in this book is set out in good faith for general guidance and no liability can be accepted for loss or expense incurred as a result of relying in particular circumstances on statements made in the book. Readers are also reminded that laws and regulations are liable to change.

Typeset by Concept Communications Ltd, Crayford, Kent.
Printed and bound by The Cromwell Press, Broughton Gifford, Melksham, Wiltshire.

Preface

Interest in French residential and commercial property has never been greater. Prices are even now generally lower than in the UK, and the French climate and culture are powerful incentives to renters and buyers.

I have sought in these pages to offer straightforward, practical and independent advice on a broad range of related subjects, based on our own direct personal experience. This include choices about buying or renting, the costs and legal processes involved, and how to avoid some of the many pitfalls.

As well as travel and holidays, Europe today offers a growing range of business opportunities. This may begin with a fact-finding mission, followed by setting up a workshop or office in France. Whilst many other books offer limited advice on domestic property, few take much account of commercial considerations. It has therefore been my intention to offer some help to those with business or professional aspirations in France, as well as to those making leisure plans.

I wish to express thanks to Rothbury's 'local hero', Mr Colin Hunter, for background research, and to my wife Maureen for helping me to maintain the balance and flow of the book.

Clive Kristen

List of Illustrations

Contents

Contents

Fig. 1. Map of France.

1
Why France?

FIRST THOUGHTS

Around half an hour is all it takes on the swiftest routes to begin experiencing something very special. There are warm summer days and lazy evenings with good food and fine wine. There is the sound of the sea and the magic of the mountains. Here is a land of history and culture with quiet country roads and busy vibrant cities. There is something for everyone to enjoy in a country where children are made as welcome as their parents. The place of course is France: it is hardly surprising that it has become the UK's most popular holiday destination.

The British invasion

It is not surprising either that more and more Britons are becoming property owners on the other side of the Channel. The idea is appealing for a number of reasons. France is our nearest neighbour, and most of us already have at least a smattering of the language. Life seems to run at an easier pace and the climate is generally better than our own. Since 1992 immigration has become easier, and the Channel Tunnel promises rapid and easy transport between the two countries. Hovercraft and SeaCat already make commuting a possibility, and high tech communication means that some kinds of business can be run effectively from any base on Europe's mainland.

Perhaps the most obvious attraction is that property prices are well below our own. It may be true that there are fewer bargains to be had these days, especially in the most popular regions, but for those who live in expensive areas of the UK the difference is still quite staggering.

LIFESTYLE

The French lifestyle is very different to our own, and there are great contrasts between city, suburban and rural areas. The overall population density is around half that of the UK but nearly three quarters of the people live in heavily industrialised urban areas. This means that French towns and cities are as busy, some say busier, than in Britain. Through vast expanses of countryside however the situation is reversed. The French call it 'la vie tranquille' and it certainly is just that.

Visitors to France often form a mistaken impression of this important difference between urban and rural life. Cities other than Paris may seem to be quieter than our own, and popular holiday resorts — especially on the coast — rather busier. This is because most visitors see France during July and August when the French themselves take their annual holidays.

The French have a high regard for intellect and education. They talk knowledgeably, even at café level, about the subtle nuances of debate in politics and religion. They are apparently gregarious, yet seem to have a dislike of formal or organised activity. These kinds of apparent contradiction make the French what they are — elusive, infuriating, introverted, intriguing, beguiling, and most frequently charming.

Culture

Culture is spelt with a capital 'C'. It is an all embracing term that reflects national achievement in art, ballet, drama, literature, music, philosophy and so on.

In recent years successive French governments have responded to criticism that Culture is elitist with projects designed to make it more accessible. The Pompidou Centre is considered to be the best free show in Paris, but typically the building itself has caused great controversy.

The French are inclined to believe that Culture is their gift to the world. Nothing is more likely to provoke argument than suggesting that perhaps Shakespeare was greater than Molière.

The Frenchman regards his Culture as a special heritage that sets him apart from lesser mortals. Cultural issues are frequently at the forefront of political and economic debate. As the great French newspaper, *Le Monde*, put it: 'the nuclear power programme has merely created controversy: the sale of national art treasures would certainly topple the government.'

The French at work

The stereotype Frenchman works extremely hard and takes his pleasures equally seriously. The working day begins early, ends late, and features a long midday break. In quieter rural areas a 'lunch hour' can stretch to 180 minutes. In the cities there has been a move towards working patterns with which we are more familiar. These include the introduction of flexitime, brief midday breaks, and the rush to beat the rush hour.

The British experience of the French at work is varied. Diplomacy is very much a French tradition and high levels of courtesy are commonplace in the world of commerce and business. Whilst eminent politicians are afforded a reverence that is rare in the UK, bureaucracy is generally treated with a disdain with which we are all too familiar. Industrial workers are renowned for a phlegmatic approach to their jobs, whilst fishermen and agricultural workers seem fiercely proud and independent.

The hotel and catering industry in France is a major employer, and standards are generally high. A 'patron' is a position of some esteem, and being a waiter is considered to be an honourable profession.

In the extensive rural areas the French worker is harder to define. By tradition, he is either helpful and friendly beyond the call of duty, or sullen and thoroughly uncooperative. Of course a great deal of this may be to do with the way he is approached by the visitor. An attempt to speak his own language, even at the most basic schoolboy level, is likely to produce the best results.

THE FRENCH CHARACTER

There is no such thing as a typical Frenchman, but there are identifiably typical French characteristics.

The family

Very large families may be a thing of the past, but the family remains the key currency of French social life. The Frenchman may be apparently friendly, but he is much more likely to invite you to an expensive restaurant than into his home. Family life is distinct and separate from everything else in his world and 'le weekend' is an institution that is still cherished.

Tradition

Despite the popular image of the great fashion houses in Paris the French are generally conservative in their dress. Indeed they are conservative in many of their attitudes and they recognise the importance of history and tradition. This is reflected in the number and variety of traditional festivals which abound throughout the year.

Regional differences

A distinction is often made between Paris and the rest of France. Sometimes it is claimed the capital is untypically French. Certainly the Parisian is different, but so is the Basque, the Breton, and the Corsican. They show different facets of a varied national character — like the Cockney, Geordie, or Gallic Scot — but they all remain discernibly French.

Manners and formality

At almost all levels of French society good manners remain the norm. This means old-fashioned formality. First name familiarity is reserved generally for close friends and relations. The handshake — or cheek kiss — is used for every meeting and farewell.

Privacy is paramount for the Frenchman. A phone call is expected before you visit a friend or neighbour, or even an associate in his office. You may enquire politely about someone's general state of health but other questions about personal life should be avoided. Safe conversational gambits include sport, the arts, the news, and of course, the weather.

It is expected that you will make regular use of a person's title — Monsieur, Madame, or Mademoiselle. If you listen to conversational French you may well think the title occurs in almost every sentence.

This kind of formality does not reflect either recent major changes in the structure of French society, or the familiar cry of 'Vive la difference'. What has happened is often compared to the iceberg. The changes have taken place beneath the surface, but the 'tip' that we observe appears to remain constant. It is also true to say that the nature of the formality is very much in keeping with the way the French prefer to keep themselves to themselves. Informality leads to intimacy: intimacy is an intrusion of privacy. That is the French equation of manners.

CLIMATE

France is the largest country in Western Europe, with considerable regional variation in climate.

We tend to think of it as being altogether warmer and sunnier than Britain as it lies to the south. This is not altogether true: Calais, for instance, is more northerly and colder and wetter than Plymouth.

Much of France lies in the Northern Temperate Zone and is affected by the prevailing westerlies of the Atlantic. The Gulf Stream plays a significant part in determining the coastal climate. Brest, in the north of Brittany, enjoys similar winter temperatures to the Mediterranean resorts. In general terms, the climate of the north and west is similar to Devon and Cornwall.

South from a line which roughly parallels the Loire, the influence of the Mediterranean increases, and the climate is generally warmer and drier. People speak of 'the pull of the Midi'. The east of the country towards the Alps has a more typically European climate with a greater variation in seasonal temperatures. Both the Alps and Pyrenees have climates which can be severe in the winter, and uncertain even in the summer months.

LANGUAGE

Largely through the influence of television the French language has become more universal and standardised. There are still however strong local variations which reflect the history and traditions of the regions. The Bretons and Basques have languages of their own which are as fiercely preserved as the Welsh tongue. There are, however, only a few isolated communities where the natives are not truly bilingual.

There is a range of dialect, too. In Alsace, for instance, the Germanic influence remains strong. There are also measured regional dialects and accents of different kinds with perhaps the 'street language' of Paris and Marseille creating the most problems for the visitor.

THE STATE

Education

France has arguably one of the finest state education systems in the world. The cornerstone of success is still the **Baccalauréat** — an educational reform instituted by Napoleon. The 'Bac' is now achieved by two thirds of French youngsters and is the key to the door of higher education. French education is also in a state of flux at present. They are looking at the possibility of moving away from a highly structured national curriculum — which states the page to be studied at a given time — towards a freer version similar to that being vilified in our own country.

Politics

The Fifth Republic, which has lasted since 1958, was essentially the creation of Charles de Gaulle.

The Head of State, who is the President, is elected by universal suffrage for a term of seven years. He selects the Prime Minister and other ministers. He is Chairman of the Cabinet, and Commander of the Armed Forces.

The Head of Government is the Prime Minister who is also the leader of the parliament. This is divided into two houses — the National Assembly and the Senate. The National Assembly, which has the power to reverse Senate's decisions, is elected by an unusual two round majority system every five years. The Senate is elected for nine years by an electoral college.

The system is complex, unwieldy and unique. Only the French could create such a hierarchy and make it work with any measure of success.

The law
Founded on the principles of the Code Napoléon for administrative justice, there are now **codes** — circulars, decrees and statutes — covering all aspects of French law.

Essentially there are two systems — the administrative and the judiciary. Administrative justice is about settling disputes between the individual and the government. The judiciary deals with civil and criminal cases.

There are levels of tribunals and courts which give French citizens high standards of legal protection. There is no jury system but a mixed tribunal of (three) professional and (six) lay judges. Four of the judges must agree to secure a conviction.

The economy
Although France has been subjected to the bite of world economic recession, price and wage controls seem to have helped to minimise unemployment and sustain a large sector of public employees.

France has an economy which is based on the bedrock of the fourth most successful industrial country in the world. Agriculture is diverse and generally efficient. Tourism is becoming increasingly important in generating vast amounts of foreign exchange.

Her future as a major economic power should remain secure if France can remain a leader in 'new' industries — such as aerospace and electronics.

TO BUY OR NOT TO BUY?

Buy in haste, repent at leisure
Buying property is the biggest single financial commitment that most people make. If that property is in another country, it is wise to be doubly sure that this obligation is understood. Awareness of possible snags and pitfalls is an important part of the process of planning the purchase. For many people it can mean the difference between pleasure of ownership and total disaster.

The British recession of the late 1980s and early 1990s means that many people are no longer in a position to afford a second home and they are having real problems selling their French home. The French property market is fairly stable and prices have not risen to enable them to recoup the cost of restoration. Others have discovered that they, or their children, have simply not settled to living the year round in a foreign country.

It is the common experience of those who have purchased property in France that they have not enjoyed the benefit of fully independent advice. For many of them the story has ended happily, and problems encountered have been fairly painlessly overcome. Others have been less fortunate and have gained little beyond an expensive lesson in life.

Consider renting first

It is highly recommended that prospective French house buyers rent property first. Short term letting, especially at peak holiday periods, can be pricy, but can also be very worthwhile. Longer term arrangements — over a period of perhaps twelve months — are well worth considering. French estate agents generally act for property owners. The lessee (person renting the property) will be offered a contract with conditions that have become standardised since the act of December 1986.

Renting has other advantages:

● You are not tying up capital or borrowing large sums of money.

● You have a chance to fully research the local property market.

● You have time to find out how well you and your family adapt to a new way of life.

A giant step

Are you ready to make the leap across the channel? It may be only 22 miles of water, but for the unprepared it can be a huge psychological and cultural barrier. There are no English subtitles on French TV and there is no *Coronation Street*.

Types of purchase
Prospective purchasers of French property often fall into one of four groups:

● A businessman 'seconded' by his company, or an entrepreneur developing his interests in the wider European market.

● A person looking for a second or holiday home.

● People wishing to retire abroad or moving to a 'better' climate for health reasons.

● Escapers, dreamers, good-lifers, and various styles and shades of creative talent.

There are no exact figures for the numbers in each category, partly because they invariably overlap. Perhaps 'someone approaching retirement who buys a second home with a view to making it a first if he can sell some paintings' is as reliable a stereotype as any.

Whatever category you place yourself in the advice remains the same: do not buy a property in France until you fully understand what you are letting yourself in for.

A second home

If you are considering a second home, but have never owned one before, ask yourself the following questions:

1. Will you get enough use from the property? A second home is an all the year round expense.

2. Will you want to spend all your holidays in the same spot?

3. Will the travelling put you off taking short breaks there?

4. What size property do you want? Do you really need five extra bedrooms for all those friends who have said they may visit?

5. How much of your holiday time are you prepared to devote to minor repairs and decorating?

6. Will you let others — for payment or not — use the property in your absence?

7. If other users pay, how will this affect your mortgage/tax position?

8. Do you need a caretaker? The times when you are not there may also be the best time for major repairs/renovations. Who will oversee them?

What arrangements need to be made for properties not in use? Britain unfortunately does not have a monopoly on crime and empty property is attractive to criminals. Any arrangements you would make to protect your home in Britain should be similarly applied in France.

It is easy to think you'll be willing to spend 'a bit' of time spring cleaning and decorating in the euphoria of a holiday, but how will you feel arriving hot, tired and thirsty after a hard week at work? Do think through the implications carefully.

Emigrating

If you're considering moving lock, stock and barrel, ask yourself these questions before you commit yourself:

- What is your chosen region like in both January and July? A chalet in the Alps may be idyllic in the late Spring, but rather less so after two weeks of heavy snow falls — especially if you don't ski.

- Do you have the full support of your family? Will your wealthy aunt cut you off without a penny now she is no longer invited for Sunday lunch?

- Have you thought through the implications for healthcare and education?

- Will you be able to work and/or transfer sufficient funds to live on?

- Is your French up to coping with everything you need to do?

Given the warnings in previous paragraphs about the potential difficulties of selling, you must be absolutely positive that the move is the right one for you.

NEED TO KNOW

Before you begin house hunting there are a number of things you need to know.

These include:

☐ Personal taxation

☐ Registration tax

☐ Capital gains tax

- ☐ Nationality and naturalisation

- ☐ Rights as a European citizen

- ☐ Working in France

- ☐ Estate agents and notaries

- ☐ Building in France

- ☐ Banking and finance

- ☐ Disputes and litigation

- ☐ Maintaining the vernacular

- ☐ The legal process of purchase

- ☐ Surveys and planning permission

- ☐ Renting and running your property

- ☐ Legal responsibilities

Later sections of this book deal with each of these.

Do not be put off by what seems to be an encyclopaedia of knowledge. The French frequently do things differently, but the approach is generally based on common sense and much of the legal process is designed to protect you.

Price pointers

The regional guide in the next chapter will be helpful, but here are some general pointers:

New/old properties

As a rule of thumb, newer properties are more expensive than older ones.

Apartments and condominiums

Brand new apartments and condominiums are particularly expensive. They are invariably built on prime sites in fashionable areas.

Older apartments and condominiums are variably priced. Much depends on the age and condition of the whole building. This is a sector of the market which requires special caution. There are bargains to be had, but mainly for experienced buyers.

Communications

Property values decrease according to their remoteness. In the same region you may find a large country house in the same price range as a seaside apartment.

Changing fashions

Regions, particularly towns and villages, and even some streets are 'fashionable'. This is always reflected in price.

Estate agents

French estate agents are well aware of the buying whims and fancies of their UK customers. In some places you will find agents with window displays in English. This is not because of the entente cordiale, but because the agents know the British are frequently foolish enough to pay the inflated asking price.

Buying direct

As French estate agents charge the seller or the buyer around 5% for their services, it is often possible to save this amount (or more) by buying direct. Local newspapers are often a good place to start for prospective buyers.

Le petit jardin

A small garden — un petit jardin — has a different meaning on each side of the channel. We tend to think of something a bit larger than a window box, they regard it as something that does not require the service of a full-time gardener.

Costs of purchase

Registration fees are lower on properties that are less than five years old. The full legal process of purchase, including perhaps surveys and planning applications, is likely to cost between 10 and 15 per cent on top of the property purchase price.

Negotiating the price

As in Britain the asking price is invariably more than the final selling price and it is difficult to judge how much room there is to negotiate. Be prepared to walk away from a deal, whilst showing some enthusiasm for the property itself. Leave a telephone number and wait for a call.

WHAT CHOICE IS THERE?

There is property in France to suit all pockets and lifestyles. The single most common type of property in all areas is the **pavillon**. This is a detached family house in a fairly large (by English standards) garden and usually with a sous-sol (underground area) that acts as a laundry room, garage and cellar.

French estate agents will willingly send out lists of properties they are marketing. Many of them place sample advertisements in English newspapers. This is not a good way to buy. The 'sample' properties have invariably been sold if you make an enquiry, but you may be inundated with details of 'selected' houses. The process of 'selection' is often related to the difficulty of selling particular properties to French buyers.

However, the estate agent's window is the prime source of information once you have made the decision to buy. Studied carefully it can tell you a great deal about a local property market.

Here are some recent examples from a French agency. The first is a property close to a pleasant market town on the banks of the Loire.

AGENTS IMMOBILIERS D'ERNEST

Maison traditionelle 130 M2, 4 chambres, cuisine equipée, salle de bains, 2 toilettes, construction de très bonne qualité, cheminée, sejour, salon, portes fenêtres aluminium, double vitrage, 2 garages, cave, grenier, terrasse 30 M2 couverts + 60 M2 non couverts, chauffage electrique, terrain 1620 M2, clos et arbores. 770,000 F.

Translation: Ernie's Estate Agency
Traditional house of 130 square metres, 4 bedrooms, fully equipped kitchen, bathroom, 2 WCs, very good quality construction, open fireplace, lounge, living room, aluminium French windows, double glazing, 2 garages, cellar, attic, 30 square metres of covered terrace with 60 square metres uncovered, electric central heating, 1620 square metres of land, walled garden with trees. £77,000 (assuming exchange rate of 10F = £1).

The second is in a small rural village about 10 miles from the same town.

Agents Immobiliers D'Ernest

150 M2, 4 chambres, cuisine equipée, 2 salles de bains, 2 toilettes, construite sur 2 niveaux, garage, sejour, salon, terrasse, chauffage electrique + cheminée, terrain de 3 acres, belle prestations, située dans l'arrière pays village historique, tous commerces, deservi par bus. 650,000 F.

Translation: Ernie's Estate Agency
150 square metres, 4 bedrooms, fully equipped kitchen, 2 bathrooms, 2 WCs, split level construction, garage, lounge, living room, terrace, electric central heating and open fireplace, 300 sq. metres of land, situated behind an historic village, local shops etc, bus service. £65,000 (assuming exchange rate of 10F = £1).

Finally, here is a property on offer close to the town centre.

Agents Immobiliers D'Ernest

90 M2, 3 chambres, cuisine equipée, salle de bains, toilette, construction de plain pied, isolation thermique et phonique, alarme, parking, chauffage electrique, adoucisseur d'eau, terrasse, terrain 135 M2, très bon état general. 620,000 F.

Translation: Ernie's Estate Agency
90 square metres, 3 bedrooms, fully equipped kitchen, bathroom, WC, natural stone construction, heat and sound insulation, alarm, parking place, electric central heating, water softener, terrace, 135 square metres of land, very good general condition. £62,000 (assuming exchange rate of 10F = £1).

Making the right choice
Within a fairly narrow price band a range of lifestyles is amply demonstrated by these three properties. Each have their own attractions so it is important that the buyer is sure exactly what he is looking for. Nothing is more likely to bring a look of despair onto a French estate agent's face than you offering him no other guideline beyond price.

In England the motto is 'you pay your money and take your choice': for the French it is very much the other way round!

2
Where and
What to Buy

Before diving into the French property market there are a number of
matters to consider.

THE REGIONS

Some buyers may have already fixed a geographical target area; others
may prefer to begin by investigating the relative merits of different
regions.

According to FNAIM (**Fédération Nationale des Agents Immobiliers**, 1991 survey) the ten most popular regions with the British are:

- The Pas de Calais and the coastal strip of Picardy around Boulogne
  and Le Touquet.

- Normandy, particularly around Deauville and Honfleur.

- Brittany, especially the coastal strips between St Malo and Roscoff,
  Quimper and Vannes.

- The Loire Valley in general, but mainly around Tours and Blois.

- Charente and Charente Maritime.

- The Dordogne.

- The Ardeche.

- Provence in general, but especially the Vaucluse and the areas around
  Nîmes and Aix-en-Provence.

- The Jura, particularly the Doubs and Loue Valleys.

- The Vosges.

Target areas

Many buyers of French property have a good idea of their target. Sometimes they have friends in a certain area, or they have already rented a gîte.

It is surprising, however, that many people do not investigate the merits of different parts of the country. Each region has its own character and climate, and each can provide a personal checklist of advantages and disadvantages.

Inland rural areas are likely to provide the greatest bargains. These are generally the parts of France where agriculture boomed and the population rose rapidly during the last two centuries. That population trend is now in reverse and there are many properties that the French themselves will not buy.

Each region offers distinctive vernacular architecture, some real bargains, especially in larger rural buildings, and various degrees of accessibility.

TARGET POINTERS

It is perhaps appropriate at this point for you to ask yourself what your priorities are. If you have not decided upon a region, your priorities and the thumbnail sketches below may well help. Try listing the phrases below in order of preference:

Preference

1. Easy access by car. _____

2. Climate is hot and sunny all year round. _____

3. Area is quiet and suitable for most country pursuits. _____

4. Plenty of cultural/historical opportunities nearby. _____

5. Close to the sea. _____

6. Close to rail/air links. _____

7. Area suitable for children. _____

8. Area appropriate for specialist hobbies eg. golf, fishing. _____

Each of the ten areas pinpointed by FNAIM has its aficionados; much depends upon your personal choice.

The Pas de Calais and Picardy

Has the recommendation of accessibility, but most visitors see only the less attractive areas around the ports of Calais and Dunkirk and from the autoroute. Of all the French regions though this is the one with the greatest intensity of British owned property. The price differential, or advantage, has eroded since the British property market went into decline. Property sales to English buyers have been described by agents as steady in recent years, following a boom period in the early and mid 1980s.

Normandy

Again the main advantage is proximity, with Cherbourg, Caen and Le Havre as the access ports. In the late 1980s many bargains were picked up by the British, particularly around Honfleur and Deauville. Both French and British builders earned a good living for some years renovating inexpensive cottages. The situation has changed recently, but there are still bargains to be had in larger properties.

Coastal property is relatively expensive apart from the Cherbourg (Cotentin) peninsula. Inland there are still bargains to be had but prices increase towards the Paris 'weekender belt'. There are some delightful pockets of countryside in inland Normandy, and bargain hunters will find properties on offer that are as good value as any in regions favoured by British buyers.

Brittany

Brittany is more difficult to access, particularly in winter, but it is still justifiably popular with British buyers. The influence of the gulf stream makes part of the coast — especially in the North West — remarkably mild for the latitude.

The area around St Malo, Dinard and Dinan is delightful, but prices reflect this popularity. There are better bargains to be had along the coast westwards towards Roscoff.

Properties in Brittany represent very good value, and the west coast area between Quimper and Vannes is a popular choice. The difference in prices between sea-view and inland properties — sometimes no more than a couple of kilometres from each other — is marked nowhere more than in southern Brittany.

The Loire Valley

The river is said to be a major climatic division of France, and it is certainly true to say that during the summer months the influence of the Midi (the south) is noticeable.

The Loire is also known as the market garden of France. It is an area rich in history vividly reflected by the magnificent chateaux. Routes to the Loire are not good from the channel ports but this does not seem to deter visitors and potential property owners.

The most popular section is the valley between Tours and Blois, and along the tributary rivers — the Cher and the Indre. Prices depend very much on precise geographical location.

Charente and Charente Maritime

An area that has opened up because of improved motorway links, and one that is becoming increasingly popular with British buyers. There is a plentiful supply of inexpensive property, and it is well worth considering for people with a limited budget.

The area around Cognac and Saintes attracts the majority of inland buyers, whilst property in the fishing ports and islands to the northwest are frequently the choice of seasonal visitors.

The Dordogne

Is one of France's longest and most beautiful rivers. The most attractive area — between Bort-les-Orgues and Beaulieu-sur-Dordogne — is also the most expensive.

More remote parts of the Limousin and Perigord, and areas closer to the volcanic region of the Auvergne, offer better bargains.

The Dordogne was one of the first areas of France to attract significant numbers of British buyers. Although there are still bargains to be found, the days of the country cottage for a few thousand pounds have long since disappeared.

The Dordogne is also known as the cauldron of France. High summer temperatures and humidity can prove to be either attractive or unbearable. The higher areas of the Auvergne offer a more temperate summer climate, but they can be bitterly cold in the winter months. Improved motorway links have made the Auvergne a recent target for bargain hunters. Property can be found that is as inexpensive as anywhere in France, but this is a thinly populated region so the buyer may find himself exploring far from the beaten track.

The Ardeche

To the north of Provence and now almost as popular. The Ardeche itself is one of the most attractive rivers in France particularly around the famous gorges.

The climate is similar to Provence and the landscape is pleasantly wooded and hilly. Although prices are not as high as Provence, properties can no longer be regarded as exceptional value.

Provence

Good motorway links have made the area accessible. However, it is the excellent year round climate, the sense of history, and the variety of landscape that makes Provence a very popular choice with British buyers.

Property prices reflect this, especially in the Vaucluse and around Nîmes and Aix-en-Provence. Provence is not an area for the bargain hunter, but it can still be regarded as remarkable value for money for buyers who are used to checking out prices in estate agents' windows in the south of England.

The Jura

More accessible than the Alps and less bleak than the Pyrenees, the Jura is quickly becoming a popular choice for buyers seeking a mountain retreat, with the added pleasure of winter sports.

With the highest peaks rising to above 1600 metres the climate can sometimes show the rawness of an upland region. It has been claimed that there are eight months of snow and two of wind but the rest of the year is wonderful. . .

There are numerous villages with country style buildings. Thanks to the limited inroads that tourism has made into the region there are also some real property bargains. The most popular areas of this region of 'Old France' are the Doubs and Loue valleys and the high valley of the Ain.

The Vosges

The Vosges again reflect the huge variety of what France offers the property buyer.

Although interest in this hilly and wooded region has increased in recent years there are still good bargains on offer. Delightful villages such as Bussang, Ferrette, Le Hohwald, St Amerin and Schirmeck vie for the attention of the buyer with the popular larger resort towns of Masevaux and Plombières les Bains.

The Vosges is particularly popular with nature lovers and walkers who enjoy peace and unspoiled countryside. The names suggest the links with Germany and this is reflected in the wine and local food.

PRICE GUIDELINES

It is impossible to be precise about how much you would expect to pay for a French property. This is because variations within regions themselves can be considerable.

The following tables may provide a valuable guideline. They summarise comprehensive returns from eight major towns and their surrounding districts. The prices are an average for various property types and are rounded to the nearest £10.

Each figure is based on one square metre of property and assumes an exchange rate of 10 francs to the pound.

It may be helpful to know that a large three/four bedroom house with a garage is likely to be around 180 square metres, a typical three bedroom bungalow around 120 square metres, and a small two bedroom bungalow around 80 square metres.

The surveys for figures 2, 3 and 4 were carried out by Macdonald Research during July and August 1991. At least three agencies in each town were asked to provide data. Information from 1,372 price returns was used to compile these tables.

Conclusions
Although there are inconsistencies, it is possible to draw the following general conclusions:

● Suburban properties are around 75% of town centre values.

● Rural properties are around 50% of town centre values.

● The cost of a new property is often almost twice the price of an unrestored one.

TOWN CENTRE PRICES

District	Unrestored	Renovated	New
Bordeaux	420	770	1200
Clermont Ferrand	510	700	950
Dijon	550	700	960
Lille	440	840	1070
Lyon	550	800	1150
Marseille	310	620	980
Nantes	410	690	990
Orléans	450	650	950
Rouen	480	790	1110
Strasbourg	500	730	1050
Average	**470**	**730**	**1040**

Fig. 2. Average town centre prices (£ per square metre at FF10/£1).

SUBURBAN PRICES

District	Unrestored	Renovated	New
Bordeaux	300	550	800
Clermont Ferrand	320	550	750
Dijon	330	430	770
Lille	310	470	750
Lyon	370	550	880
Marseille	240	350	720
Nantes	310	480	750
Orléans	380	570	750
Rouen	390	550	820
Strasbourg	350	500	810
Average	**330**	**500**	**780**

Fig. 3. Average suburban prices (£ per square metre, at FF10/£1).

RURAL PRICES

District	Unrestored	Renovated	New
Bordeaux	220	390	630
Clermont Ferrand	240	370	510
Dijon	260	340	540
Lille	210	430	550
Lyon	290	420	670
Marseille	170	330	550
Nantes	220	340	530
Orléans	210	330	480
Rouen	310	390	590
Strasbourg	280	370	570
Average	**240**	**370**	**560**

Fig. 4. Average rural prices (£1 per square metre at FF10/£1).

Stability

Price stability is predicted to continue throughout 1993 and possibly beyond.

The French property market has not experienced the rapid spirals of price inflation that took place in the UK during the 1970s and 80s. Prices tend to ease forward gradually in line with building costs, wages, and the general state of the economy. Even the French economy has been in recession recently.

3
Renting a Property and Timeshare

Holidays spent in hotels and guest houses can help you decide if an area is suitable for you, as can renting a property.

HOTELS AND GUEST HOUSES

Hotels in France charge around half as much for a room as you would expect to pay in the UK for two people sharing a room. A hotel — particularly in rural areas — can be easier on the pocket than a gîte.

Look out for the sign **Chambre(s) à Louer** hanging in the windows of ordinary domestic property. If the sign is displayed then a room is available, often at a price that would be considered uneconomic in the UK.

It is a French tradition that you are shown accommodation before you decide whether or not to sign the register. This applies to hotels, guest houses, or even a spare bedroom in somebody's home. French law requires that prices of all hotel rooms must be displayed in a prominent place, with minimum and maximum guidelines on the outside of the building.

Lists and details of all available accommodation can be obtained at the local syndicat d'initiative.

HOLIDAY LETTING

Gîtes (holiday properties) are advertised in many national UK news-papers.

Gîtes provide furnished self-catering accommodation that can be any-thing from a château to a farmhouse or a seaside apartment. They are classified according to the facilities they provide and each local **syndicat d'initiative** (tourist information office) retains a list of properties avail-able in the area. A national Federation imposes rules about minimum standards of furnishing and facilities.

The best way of finding a good gîte is frequently through personal recommendation. Be wary of newspaper advertisements. Some of those that appear to offer particular gîtes are in fact 'samples' placed by letting agencies. The gîte advertised is not usually available, and indeed may not even exist. What you will receive however is a wad of unsolicited mail frequently offering inferior quality accommodation at grossly inflated prices.

Most reputable companies issue information brochures. *Blakes Villas Country Holidays in France, The Complete France* and *Vacances en Campagne* can normally be obtained through UK travel agents. These companies can be regarded as specialists offering a wide selection of accommodation at competitive rates. Brittany Ferries also offer a wide range of packages which include gîte rental, ferry and so on.

France Magazine, a quarterly publication which can be obtained through newsagents, is a source of valuable advice. It also includes listings of quality gîtes, many of which are being offered for the first time during the forthcoming season.

Gîtes de France

Bookings can be made through the London office of **Gîtes de France**. This is a national organisation which issues up to date lists of accommodation, prices, and availability. The advantage of booking in this way is that the whole transaction can be carried out in English.

Good self catering accommodation is sometimes difficult to find because the French themselves seek out the best for their own holidays.

Local tourist offices

Local tourist offices are always willing to send out extensive lists of all forms of accommodation available.

It is worthwhile restricting any enquiry to the kind of accommodation you require.

Sample Letter
Syndicat D'Initiative,
4500 St. Pierre-en-Laye,
France.

15th April 1993

Messieurs,

Veuillez m'envoyer une liste des gîtes à louer avec les tarifs.

Veuillez accepter l'expression de mes sentiments distingués.

Translation

Tourist Information Office,
4500 St. Pierre-en-Laye,
France.

15th April 1993

Dear Sirs,

Please send me details of holiday properties available for letting together with a price list.

Yours faithfully,

Fig. 5. Enquiry letter in French/English.

Booking direct

This is often the cheapest way of reserving a gîte. The problem is that the information you receive from the owner may be sketchy, and in high season the best gîtes are frequently reserved from one year to the next.

For your protection it is always best to get a written agreement. Some gîte owners send out printed forms.

Points to check

It is important to be sure about:

● The duration of the let and times of arrival and departure.

● The deposit. Normally 10% but some owners demand up to 25%.

● Arrangements for the payment of services — electricity, water etc.

● The facilities — particularly the numbers of beds and bedrooms.

● Exactly what is provided as part of the letting 'package'.

● Arrangements for car parking. Many apartments are allocated off-road parking for one vehicle.

● Arrangements for picking up and returning keys.

Advance payments

The deposit paid for a gîte is either **un acompte** or **arrhes**. The legal distinction is important.

If you cancel after having paid 'un acompte' you not only lose the deposit but the gîte owner can hold you responsible for the full amount due for the letting period.

If you cancel having paid 'arrhes' only the deposit is forfeited.

However, this does not always mean that it is best to have the deposit described as 'arrhes'. 'Un acompte' means you can make a claim for breach of contract if the gîte is unsatisfactory, or if you are denied access. Depending on circumstances the damages awarded could be considerable. 'Arrhes' under French law means that the gîte owner will be obliged to pay only twice the deposit you gave him.

The best advice when booking direct is to pay 'un acompte' but to ensure that you have holiday insurance that covers you if you are unable to travel.

Tax incentives for gîte owners

There are tax incentives for owners to offer properties as a gîte. In order to qualify the gîte has to be available for at least three months of the year.

It is not uncommon for the owner to make the accommodation available only for the summer season. This is because he can obtain maximum revenue for the least inconvenience. Rental prices in winter are barely half of what is demanded in July and August. A gîte may be part of a house — an annexe or a granny flat for instance — that returns to regular use for the rest of the year.

Gîtes may be good value for a large family, or shared with friends, but they can be prohibitively expensive for a single person or a couple.

LONG TERM LETTING

Acts passed in 1986 and 1989 mean that a standard contract — **Contrat de Location** — applies to all lettings of more than three months duration. This contract clearly sets our all the rights and responsibilities of landlord and tenant.

The lease

Landlord and tenant are required to hold copies of the contract. This document includes 12 key clauses:

CONTRAT DE LOCATION

Loi No. 89-462 du 6 juillet 1989

LOCAUX VACANTS NON MEUBLES

Entre les soussignés

BAILLEUR *(Property owner)* . . . .
. . . .

MANDATAIRE *(Agent/Valuer)* . . . .
. . . .

et
LOCATAIRES *(Tenants)* . . . .
. . . .
Le baileur loue les locaux et équipements ci-après désignés au locataire qui les ac-
cepte aux conditions suivantes.
*(The owner rents the premises & equipment designated hereafter to the tenant
who accepts them subject to the following conditions.)* :

LOCAUX *(Premises)* . . . .
. . . .

. . . . . . *Habitation principale*
. . . . . . *Professionnel et Habitational principale*
. . . . . . *Appartement* . . . . . . *Maison individuelle*

DESIGNATION DES LOCAUX ET EQUIPEMENTS PRIVATIFS . . . .
. . . .

Garage No. . . . . . .   *Place de station No.* . . . . . .
Cave no. . . . . . .   *Autre* . . . . . .

ENUMERATION DES PARTIES ET EQUIPEMENT COMMUNS

. . . . . . *Gardiennage*   . . . . . . *Vide-ordures*
. . . . . . *Interphone*   . . . . . . *Ascenseur*
. . . . . . *Antenne TV collective*   . . . . . . *Chauffage collectif*
. . . . . . *Eau chaude collective*   . . . . . . *Espace(s) vert(s)*

FIXATION DU LOYER

*(Here follows a series of legal definitions of the property and its state of repair
according to articles 17, 17B and 18 of the law. If in any doubt, consult your
solicitor)*

DUREE INITIALE DU CONTRAT *(Initial period of contract)*
. . . .

RAISONS PROFESSIONNELLES OU FAMILIALES DU BAILLEUR
(Professional or family reasons for contract being less than 3 years)
. . . .
. . . .

DATE DE PRISE D'EFFET *(Date contract comes into effect)*
. . . .

Fig. 6. Model letting contract (Contrat de Location).

MONTANTS DES PAIEMENTS (Total amount of payments)

Loyer mensuel   *(Monthly rent)*   . . . .
Taxes   *(Taxes)*   . . . .
                                         . . . .
Provisions sur charges   . . . .
(Provision for charges)
Total Mensuel   *(Monthly total)*   . . . .

TERMES DE PAIEMENT   *(Payment terms)*

Cette somme sera payable d'avance et en totalité le . . . .
de chaque mois.
    (This sum will be payable in full and in advance on the . . . .
of each month.)

REVISION DE LOYER   (Rent review)

Le loyer sera revisée chaque année le . . . .
    (The rent review takes place each year in . . . . *)*

DEPOT DE GARANTIE   *(Deposit)* . . . .

CLAUSE PARTICULIERE   *(Special clause)* . . . .
. . . .
. . . .

HONORAIRES A PARTAGER PAR MOITIE
    (Fees to be equally divided)

HONORAIRES DE TRANSACTION   *(Transaction fees)*   . . . .
HONORAIRES DE REDACTION   *(Drafting fees)*   . . . .
FRAIS D'ETAT DES LIEUX   *(Local fees)*   . . . .

DOCUMENTS ANNEXES   *(Appendices)*

(These could include lists of locally defined charges, extracts from the regulations governing co-ownership, local regulations for the recovery of keys and references to neighbourhood rents.)

CLES REMISES   *(Keys)*

Nombres de clés remises au locataire   . . . .
    (Number of keys given to tenant)

SIGNATURE DES PARTIES

Fait et signé à . . . . le . . . .
en . . . . originaux dont un remis à chacun des parties qui le
reconnait.

. . . . LE BAILLEUR

. . . . LE(S) LOCATAIRE(S)

. . . .

. . . . LA CAUTION

Fig. 6. Continued.

CONDITIONS GENERALES

A. CONTRAT D'UNE DUREE MINIMALE DE 3 OU 6 ANS
(Contract for a minimum of 3 or 6 years)

* RESILIATION – CONGE   *(Termination of Lease)*

The TENANT must give a minimum of 3 months' notice, in writing. This can be reduced to 1 month in the case of loss of employment or the poor health of a tenant over 60.

The OWNER must give a minimum of 6 months' notice, in writing. This can be reduced in the event of the tenant not carrying out his legal obligations.

* RENOUVELLEMENT   *(Renewal)*

Six months before the end of the contract, the owner can propose the renewal of contract in writing.

Either: (a) For less time, but a minimum of 1 year, under same conditions as previously.

           (b) For a minimum of 3 or 6 further years under conditions to be agreed.

B. CONTRAT D'UNE DUREE INFERIEURE DE 3 ANS
(Contract for less than 3 years)

This contract is for a period of not less than 1 year. This form of contract can only be effected if the owner can prove family or professional reasons why it should be so. These reasons must be given in the contract.

CLAUSE PARTICULIERE CONCERNANT LES LOCAUX CONSTRUITS AVANT DE 1.9.1948
(Clause only for properties constructed before 1.9.48)

This deals with the state of repair of the property and the minimum standards that must be maintained.

CHARGES   *(Charges)*

This clause permits the owner to recover from the tenant such charges as repairs to communal equipment, and taxes which correspond to services from which the tenant benefits. They are to be fixed annually.

The owner must provide the tenant with a full breakdown of the charges at least one month before they are due.

Fig. 6. Continued.

DEPOT DE GARANTIE   (Deposit)

The deposit may not exceed the agreed figure for 2 monhts' rent. This amount
must be returned to the tenant not more than 2 months after the keys have been returned to the owner.

As in English law, the deposit can be used to pay any debts left behind by the tenant etc.

TRAVAUX EVENTUELS ENTRAINANT MODIFICATION DE LOYER
(Work which could lead to the modification of the rent.)

(a)   Work done by the tenant to ensure that the property remains up to minimum
      standards.

(b)   Improvements made by the owner.

OBLIGATION DU BAILLEUR   *(Owner's responsibilities)*

This includes such things as keeping theproperty in a good state of repair and
keeping receipts for payments and charges.

OBLIGATIONS DU LOCATAIRE   *(Tenant's responsibilities)*

Including such things as making due payments, keeping the property in good
order and permitting access by the owner or his appointed agent at an agreed time.

CLAUSE RESOLUTOIRE ET CLAUSE PENALE
(Penalty & termination clauses)

The main termination clause permits the owner to terminate the contract after 2
months non-payment of rent.

The main penalty clause permits the owner to recover the cost of an expulsion
order against the tenant.

SOLIDARITE INDIVISIBILITE – ELECTION DE DOMICILE

The contract is legally binding upon the heirs of either or both parties.

FRAIS – HONORAIRE   *(Fees)*

All fees are joint responsibility.

Fig. 6. Continued.

- The letting period and commencement date.

- An accurate description of the premises.

- The identification of common or shared parts of the building.

- The rental terms and payment intervals.

- A record of guarantee deposits which must not be more than the sum of two months rental.

- The proportion of service charges and local rates payable by landlord and tenant.

- The amount of tax payable on leasing. This is called **le droit de bail**.

- The responsibilities of landlord and tenant for maintenance and repair.

- Limitations applied to the use of the building.

- An inventory of fixtures and fittings.

- Penalty clauses relating to non payment of rent.

- Conditions and consents required for sub-letting.

If the property is co-owned, additional information is contained in a separate document, **Le Règlement de Co-propriété**, which sets out any special terms and conditions.

Legal and technical terms

Bail	Lease to tenant
Bailleur	Owner or landlord
Charges	Electricity, water, insurance etc.
Chauffage collectif	Communal/shared heating
Clause particulière	Special conditions
Dépôt de Garantie	The guarantee deposit
Durée Initiale	Agreed term of lease
Eau chaude collectif	Share hot water supply
Entre	(agreement) between

Durée initiale	Initial period of lease
Huissier	Bailiff and process server
Indivision	Joint ownership
Locotaire	Tenant
Loyer	Rent
Mandataire	Representative or agent
Occupation	Occupant of premises
Parties communes	Shared/common parts of the building
Parties privatives	Parts of the building in private use
Révision de loyer	Review/change of rental payments
Renouvellement	Renewal (of lease contract)
Soussigné(s)	The undersigned
Travaux	Work carried out on the building

Legal protection of the tenant

French law is said to favour the tenant over the landlord. Many aspects of the lease confirm this view.

Costs

The costs of setting up the lease agreement must be shared between landlord and tenant.

Rent reviews

If the lease contains a rent review clause it can only be exercised once annually.

Rent increases

Any changes in the rent charged cannot be greater than the government's Cost of Construction Index figure.

Maintenance and repairs

Disputed claims about responsibility for maintenance and repairs can be referred to an independent bailiff (**huissier**). His report will be accepted by the court. This generally means that a landlord is forced to carry out necessary repairs.

Tenure

The tenant will have security of tenure for a minimum of 36 months. The only exception is a provision for repossession for 'family' or 'professional' reasons. Courts take a dim view of landlords who try to apply this clause unfairly.

Notice

The tenant is required only to give three months' notice. In the case of a person becoming unemployed or finding a new job the requirement is only one month.

If the landlord requires vacant possession he must inform the tenant in writing six months before the lease expires. If this does not occur it is assumed that the lease will be further renewed for a minimum period of another 36 months.

Payments

The tenant cannot be required to pay his rent by direct debit. Although he must take out insurance, he is free to take this business to a company of his choice.

Inspections

The tenant cannot be required to make the property available for inspection at the weekend. Inspections must be of no more than two hours.

Penalties

The lease may have penalty clauses applied to non payment of rent or service charges but not for the breach of any other obligation.

INSTALMENT PURCHASE

A peculiarly French arrangement, which allows you to rent property whilst also buying some of the equity value is called **location-vente**. There are no parallels in English property transactions, though some housing associations are now encouraging a different type of shared equity scheme.

There are two methods of location vente.

Promesse unilaterale de vente

The vendor company lets a house or apartment in the normal way but included with the lease is a promise to sell — the **promesse unilaterale de vente**.

The tenant pays a higher rent than usual, which includes an element towards an agreed purchase price. An initial time period is fixed. This is generally two or three years.

This method is traditionally offered by property developers during slump periods. The main advantage to the tenant is that it allows him to fully assess the property before purchase. It is also invariably cheaper than paying a substantial mortgage.

The disadvantage is that the tenant is only likely to acquire a small equity (between 3 and 5 per cent) during the contract term. If he then decides to buy, this amount is, in effect, deducted from the purchase price. If he decides against buying he loses all the money he has paid.

Perhaps this is best seen as a letting arrangement dressed up as a purchase. For English buyers it is not recommended.

Achat en Viager

By this method the purchaser pays a substantial 'rent' for an indeterminate period of time before acquiring the property.

Again, two contracts are combined. One of these is for a sale, and the other sets up a life annuity with the vendor as named beneficiary. This annuity is the **achat en viager**.

When the sales contract is drawn up the property is valued. The annuity is determined on actuarial (insurance) scales according to the vendor's life expectancy. The greater the expectancy, the lower the annuity payments will be.

This method is employed by specialist lawyers whose clients are elderly, and have no dependant relatives or children.

Entering into any contract of this type is, in essence, a gamble. The purchaser is effectively paying an income to the vendor (or vendors) in exchange for certain rights of inheritance.

The achat en viager has a passing resemblance to the **tontine**, still legal in France but outlawed in the UK. Here a named survivor (often one of several named) inherits the property. This is a contract that can literally lead to murder.

The achat en viager should be regarded with equal caution.

TIMESHARE

Bi-propriété

Whilst the semi-detached house is a largely British institution, bi-propriété is characteristically French.

The French own more second homes pro rata than any other nation in Europe. The bi-propriété boom began to decline a generation ago. Its popularity was based on a simple financial formula that provided substantial holiday residences for large families. Typically two senior family members (often brothers) would buy a seaside or country house and share the use of it.

The right to enjoy the property was technically divided over six month periods. The responsibilities of each shareholder (co-owner) were set out in contract.

The arrangement worked well in most cases through family cooperation and informal flexibility. During the summer months extended family groups would often meet under the shared roof. Half shares in the property were generally passed on from one generation to the next.

Bi-propriété is now something of a rarity. Smaller family units are more independent and they require less spacious accommodation. The second home is now more likely to be a seaside apartment or condominium — much less suitable for a bi-propriété arrangement.

Bi-propriété leaves behind it a legacy of difficulties created when shares in the property were passed beyond the family. The share value of one half of the bi-propriété is generally worth only about 40% of the whole property's nominal value.

Multi-propriété

What we know as timeshare the French call multi-propriété. Although we may regard it as a long-term rental agreement for a particular property (normally a designated apartment), the word propriété means ownership.

This is stressed by marketing men. They also use such terms as inter-propriété, poly-propriété, and pluri-propriété, and sometimes you will hear multi-propriété called **multi-vacances** (literally many holidays) in order to encourage an impression of the recreational nature of the purchase.

Timeshare has not enjoyed a good press, and the variety of terms used to describe it begins to explain why. Even France's finest legal minds have become confused about the legal status of some timeshare agreements.

The difficulty arises because of what is actually bought. All timeshare owners purchase a **jouissance** — a right to occupy and enjoy a property at designated times. Others (mainly since 1986) have also become part of a **société civile** — a company that holds voting shares in the property. This is intended to give them a say in the way the property is managed. In practice though, as timeshare 'owners' are often scattered around a dozen countries, the management function is generally performed by an agent whose decisions may be totally arbitrary.

Timeshare purchasers have now rather more rights, but confusions in legal terminology means that some of them have also acquired more responsibilities. This partly explains why few pre-1986 purchasers have opted to form a société civile.

Multi-propriété has its aficionados who claim it is a way of enjoying a holiday home at a modest price.

Before purchasing timeshare ask yourself the following questions:

- How much does the timeshare really cost? Budget annually, and remember to count service, maintenance, and administration charges. Compare this figure to the rental of a comparable gîte for the same time period.

- Is the purchase a good investment? Marketing leaflets are likely to make this claim but some owners have lost money on re-sale.

- What procedures are there for resolving disputes? Any multi-occupied building has potential problems. Timeshare, by its very nature, has more potential users than most.

- What rights do you have to sub-let, or to re-assign your rights to others? Problems can occur with inherited timeshares, especially when there has been more than one signatory to an agreement.

- What are the arrangements for the maintenance of the building? Where timeshare purchasers are designated as co-owners the ultimate responsibility is theirs. A poorly maintained building will lose value and is more likely to be subject to vandalism.

- Are carpets, curtains, fixtures and fittings replaced systematically and regularly? There is evidence to suggest that equipment in multi-occupied apartments will wear out approximately three times more quickly than usual.

4
Settling in France

INITIAL DOCUMENTATION

Although EC regulations have reduced the amount of documentation required for longstay visitors to member countries there are still a number of requirements in force.

Passport
A standard British passport is valid for ten years and a visitors passport for one year only.

No visa is required for tourists staying in France for up to three months. A person who stays for longer than three months is classified as a resident. He must first have an extended visa, then a resident's permit.

Visa de Longue Durée
Apply to the French consulate nearest your home for a **visa de longue durée** (long stay visa). You need proof of identity, photographs, evidence that you will have somewhere to stay in France, and proof of means of support. In practical terms this last requirement is generally satisfied by a letter from your bank, together with a translation.

People owning property in France have to provide a copy of the title of ownership. For spouses of French nationals a copy of the marriage certificate is required. All documents must be produced in duplicate together with a valid ten year passport.

You will be asked to fill in six duplicate (application) forms. A passport photograph should be attached to each.

According to consular guidelines you should allow four to five months for processing. In practice it normally takes four to six weeks. Though consulates are not noted for processing applications at high speed, it is surprising what they can achieve in a real emergency.

There are four French consulates in the UK, Edinburgh, Jersey, Liverpool and London. Their addresses are:

21 Cromwell Rd
London SW7
Tel: (071) 581 5292

Cunard Buildings
Pier Head
Liverpool L3 1ET
Tel: (051) 236 1156

La Mothe St
St Helier
Jersey
Tel: (0534) 26256

11 Randolph Crescent
Edinburgh EH3 7TT
Tel: (031) 225 7954

Carte de Séjour

The second phase is to apply for a **carte de séjour** or resident's permit. Once you are in France you should take your visa to the mairie, sous préfecture (or préfecture in a large town) and ask for a carte de séjour.

There are three months allowed to convert your visa de longue durée to a carte de séjour.

This is normally a straightforward process as long as the préfecture is satisfied that the visa is in good order. Unfortunately there are cases where local officials can be obstructive.

Should a difficulty occur the following organisations have great experience in sorting out documentation:

British Embassy
35 Rue de Faubourg St Honoré
75008 Paris
Tel: (1) 42.66.91.42.

British Council
9 Rue de Constantine
75007 Paris
Tel: (1) 42.89.11.11.

Alliance Française
101 Boulevard Raspail
75006 Paris
Tel: (1) 45.44.38.28.

French citizenship
Some property owners may consider applying for French citizenship. You are required to:

- have lived in France for at least five years. For the spouses of people who already hold French citizenship and their children this regulation does not apply;

- be more than 18 years of age;

- have no criminal record in France or the UK;

- prove that you can speak and write in French to a reasonable standard.

MANAGING THE REMOVAL

Moving within the UK can be a stressful experience. Taking your property to France can be doubly so.

A DIY removal is not recommended. Larger UK companies now have a great deal of experience of the process. Although employing this expertise can be pricy, it is nevertheless recommended. Do get more than one (written) quote and be absolutely sure what is being offered for the price quoted.

Import regulations
Household goods and personal effects can normally be imported into France duty free. Nevertheless there are a number of regulations, the breach of any of which can create considerable delay.

- Firearms may not be imported unless a special application has been processed. Details are available from consulates.

- A full inventory of goods (three copies) should be presented to customs officers when the first goods are taken to France. Property can then be imported in 'lots' but there is a time limitation (before import tax is imposed) of 12 months.

- Goods should correspond to the financial status of the owner. Customs will be suspicious of someone with a modest declared income importing a valuable collection of antiques. It is prudent to provide some form of proof of purchase for items of exceptional value.

- You will require a change of residence certificate from the mairie of the district you are moving to.

- A declaration of **non-cession** (non-transfer) is required. This is a statement that your household goods come within the duty free regulations.

- If your French property is to be used essentially as a holiday home or secondary residence additional rules apply.

It is these last rules that most frequently cause difficulty. Basically they state that all goods must have been owned and used by the importer for three months before the removal date and that they should be appropriate for usage in a secondary residence. The French would naturally prefer you to buy your goods in their country and they have been known to discourage imports. As most furniture and electrical goods are cheaper in the UK there is a natural temptation to take in as much as you can.

The best way to avoid problems is to make purchases four to six months before import and to keep receipts. Electrical goods, especially if presented to customs in original packing, are most likely to provoke comment.

Insurance

Premiums from UK insurers vary between one and two per cent of the value of the goods imported. Lower premiums cover fire, loss and theft. More comprehensive policies include accidental damage and breakages.

PETS

Despite forecasts of a relaxation in the rabies laws there are not immediate British government plans to introduce new legislation. All pets returning to the UK remain subject to six months quarantine.

Imports to France

You are allowed to import up to three domestic animals into France, but only one of them may be a puppy or an animal under six months old.

You must either provide evidence that your UK district is rabies free, or have a certificate of rabies vaccination for each animal. The vaccination is a safer bet, but a certified translation may be required.

On arrival, you are obliged to inform French customs of your intention to import an animal. To prevent any delay the necessary documentation should be easily accessible.

Rules on animal imports are likely to change at short notice. The Ministry of Agriculture suggest that you write to them around three to four weeks before departure to ask for a copy of current regulations. The address is:

Ministry of Agriculture
Animal Health Division
Export Section
Hook Rise
Tolworth
Surbiton
Surrey.

French law requires dogs to have annual anti-rabies vaccinations. The number of the certificate must be tattooed into the dog's ear. The expense of these vaccinations is one reason why this law is frequently broken. Periodic clampdowns by the authorities are received with similar fortitude to the presence of a television detector in a UK town. Prosecutions are relatively few, but penalties are severe.

The date at which a French vaccination certificate is required is twelve months from the issue of the UK equivalent, and not as popularly thought twelve months after the animal is imported to France.

HEALTH CARE

Your requirements will depend on the amount of time you intend to spend in France. Visitors who intend to stay for up to twelve months are covered by EC reciprocal arrangements with the UK. Those who intend to be resident in France should seek a more permanent solution.

Short stay

You should get form E111 from your post office. This must be filled in, signed, and stamped at the counter.

The E111 entitles you to go to any doctor or dentist in France who is a member of the state healthcare scheme. The form should last indefinitely, but a new one is required after each claim. Form E111 also entitles you to emergency hospital treatment. Some visitors to Europe, however, have reported a reluctance on the part of medical practitioners to accept E111's which are more than twelve months old.

Bills are generally sent to patients on completion of treatment. Most medical practitioners take a photocopy of E111 and reclaim their fees from the reciprocal scheme. You are still likely to have to find around 25% of the cost.

In theory you can be charged for the full cost of treatment. If this happens you are required to pay immediately. The silver lining is that E111 entitles you to reclaim the full amount. It is worth noting:

● The claim should be made before returning to the UK, and as soon as possible after treatment date.

● You will have to provide receipts for treatments and medicines and apply to the local sickness insurance fund. The address will be listed in the T2 booklet normally issued with E111.

● You can apply for compensation in the UK. One problem with this is that fund administrators have been known to apply time limits to claims. If you require treatment and do not have an E111, one can be sent to you by getting in touch with Newcastle Benefits Directorate. Tel: (091) 213 5000.

Medicines

Short stay visitors (those who have not applied for a visa de longue durée) should take an adequate supply of regularly required medication with them. Each medicine should be labelled with both its generic and trade name and dosages should be clearly indicated.

NHS doctors are strongly encouraged to supply only limited quantities of medicines. If you intend to be out of the UK for more than a month you will need certificate E112 to get further supplies in France. Enclose a covering letter from your doctor and write to:

International Relations Unit
Department of Health
Room 318
Hannibal House
Elephant and Castle
London
SE1 6TE.

Some pharmaceutical products are marketed in France with different brand names and others are formulated slightly differently. In some cases (particularly for patients suffering from a heart condition) it is best to arrange for a regularly imported supply of medication. Doctors can give long-term prescriptions to UK pharmacists who can arrange for dispatch in sealed packaging together with the appropriate customs declaration. You should expect to pay around £2 extra per package in addition to normal prescription charges.

Mail delivery times between France and the UK are notoriously irregular. It may be wise to retain several days emergency supply of regularly used medication.

English speaking doctors

Serious problems can arise because of language difficulties.

The **International Association for Medical Assistance to Travellers** (IAMAT) have a list of the 30 or so English-speaking doctors resident in France who undertake to charge fixed fees for their services. Further information can be obtained from:

IAMAT
17 Gotthardstrasse
6300 Zug
Switzerland.

British consulates also retain lists of English-speaking doctors.

Emergency help

The UK based **AA St John Alert** has access to a panel of doctors and consultants in France who can advise on any medical emergency. Help and advise is not restricted to members of the AA. There is a 24 hour emergency phone number (0256) 24872, or write to:

AA St John Alert
Fanum House
Basingstoke
Hants RG21 2BR.

Dental and eye care

French dentists and opticians are said to be amongst the best qualified in Europe.

Replacing spectacles and contact lenses is straightforward if you have a copy of your prescription. Failing that one phone call or fax to the UK can quickly remedy the situation. A new eye test will be automatically carried out if the prescription is more than five years old (three years for those over 70 years of age).

There is a special 'dial a dentist' service for emergency home treatment, and for those staying in temporary accommodation. Charges are made and reclaimed in the same way as for other medical services.

HEALTH CARE FOR RESIDENTS

If you become resident in France you can choose to make voluntary contributions to the **Securité Sociale** which administers the French Health Service. If you are retired (and in receipt of the UK state pension) you are automatically entitled to health care without making a contribution.

Form E121 is required to prove this entitlement.

Choosing a doctor

As in the UK you are theoretically entitled to choose your own medical practitioner. In practice this may also mean registering at a local health centre or clinic.

However French doctors are more likely than their UK counterparts to be working independently. Some are similar to our GPs, but the majority offer an additional specialist qualification as well. Specialist work is the most lucrative so French practitioners make a concerted effort to promote this area of their work.

Choosing a doctor is therefore not as straightforward as in the UK. *Yellow Pages* may help, but personal recommendation is likely to be better.

Signing on

Take family documentation to the **Relations Internationales Department** of the Securité Sociale. This should include passports and marriage certificates including translations.

The Relations Internationales Department is unable to recommend any individual doctor or practice. They do however provide information about many aspects of healthcare, and they hold lists of practitioners together with their specialisms.

The system

Some medical services are free of charge but others are only partially covered by the Securité Sociale.

By French law those who charge must advertise their scales of charges. It is normally possible to reclaim around 75 per cent of any charges made.

The claim is made by submitting a receipt form — the **feuille de soins**.

Most French towns have a **hôpital conventioné** which will provide a limited range of free medical services.

Medical insurance

The French private health scheme is called the **mutuelle**. By joining you can reclaim any payment you have made for medical charges. In effect you are claiming back from the Health Service the difference of approximately 25 per cent of total treatment charges that you have had to find from your own pocket. In certain circumstances (such as disability) it is possible to claim a supplementary or top up pension.

Again the Relations Internationales Department will be able to explain the rules to you.

The French Securité Sociale is really a network of organisations that provide welfare benefits. These are more extensive than their UK equivalents. To join the scheme is expensive, so private medical insurance is well worth considering. This is often cheapest and simplèst to arrange in the UK. However, insurers may question a claim made from France unless you make your intentions clear on the proposal form. It is also worth checking the wording of the policy for limitations and exclusions sometimes applied to extended illnesses and chronic medical problems.

EDUCATION

Although the French education system has become one of the most widely respected in Europe, many overseas residents choose to leave their youngsters in school on the UK mainland or elsewhere.

The alternatives

- A French public school.

- A French private school.

- An English-speaking private school.

- A bilingual school.

'Public' means a 'state' school in France. This may be considered as a good option for younger children. Studies have shown that most youngsters under 8 years of age acquire a competence in the language within three months and fluency within six. At age 11 competence comes within six months but fluency can take a year. The clear message is that the age of the child is a key factor in his ability to adapt and fully benefit from learning through the medium of a new language.

Private education is less common than in the UK, and these establishments often reflect the best and the worst in educational standards. Most of these schools are state aided and are found in the traditionally Catholic parts of the country — the Auvergne, Brittany, and Savoie. Parents considering this option should take good advice and inspect the school thoroughly themselves.

There are very few English speaking private schools. The reputable ones have high standards and competition for places is very severe.

There are also a few bilingual schools. The best ones are large, successful, and based in the capital. There is heavy competition for places.

In rural areas parents are more likely to find state schools willing to take English-speaking youngsters. Public schools are not obliged to take anyone who cannot demonstrate reasonable standards of spoken and written French.

The system

Education throughout France is notionally free, but students have to buy their own textbooks and stationery. Emphasis is on hard work, the growth of personal responsibility, and fierce competition.

The system begins at three years of age at an **Ecole Maternelle** (kindergarten). This is followed by the **Ecole Primaire** (primary school) and the **College d'Enseignment Secondaire**. The best pupils are selected from the CES to attend a **Lycée** which leads to the internationally recognised Baccalauréat standard. The 'Bac' is generally the entrance ticket to university and higher education. Beyond this the Grandes Ecoles (postgraduate study centres) offer the route to success in the professions and in the upper reaches of the civil service.

Bursaries and grants are available for higher education, but these are normally paid in the form of scholarships to needy or exceptionally gifted youngsters. French law obliges parents to leave these gifted youngsters in the education system until they have passed their 20th birthday.

The different ethos of French schools can be summarised by the attitude to truancy. In France this is a serious offence that can lead to expulsion for the child and hefty fines for the parents. It is worth noting that teachers have much greater status in the public eye than their UK counterparts.

Useful addresses

French Embassy Cultural Section
22 Wilton Crescent
London SW1X 8SB.
Tel: (071) 235 8080
General advice.

Service National d'Accueil aux Etudiants Etrangers
69 Quai D'Orsay
75007 Paris.
All aspects of student life, particularly those relating to higher education.

Service d'Information des Familles
277 Rue St Jacques
75005 Paris.
Tel: (1) 43.29.12.77.
School directories and general guidance.

Centre National de Documentation sur L'Enseignment Privé
20 Rue Faubert
75007 Paris.
Tel: (1) 47.05.32.68.
Free advice about private schooling. The most extensive descriptions of private schools and their facilities available.

UTILITIES

Electricity
French electricity is the cheapest in Europe. Standards of insulation for new property are high, and the climate is generally warmer than our own. Electricity is therefore the most popular form of domestic fuel.

The price for electricity depends on the tariff option you choose. Leaflets explaining the alternatives are issued when each new installation is made and when a new customer account is opened. They are also available on demand from any office of Electricité de France.

The present price for electricity based on 'average' household (a six kilowatt installation) is:

● 74 centimes per kilowatt hour

- a standing charge of 48 francs a month

- Off-peak tariff (**tariff avec heurs creusés**) is 60 centimes during normal hours, 30 centimes during off-peak hours, and a monthly standing charge of 30 francs.

- Local taxes add between 0 and 12 per cent to the net bill, which excludes the TVA (VAT) included in the above figures.

(The statistics are from a 1991 Electricité de France report.)

Under French law any new building or flat can be joined to the mains system. The developer has the responsibility of making sure that a building conforms to the regulations and that the appropriate certificate (**certificat de conformité**) is issued for new property. This is handed over to Electricité de France.

A deposit is required which is refunded in portions after five and ten years. A second nominal charge is made for the meter when it is connected to the supply. In some circumstances a bond is required that can be set against future electricity bills.

Though supplies and installations may be cheap, safety standards are not what we have come to expect in the UK. Watch out for:

- Insufficient power points, particularly in the kitchen.

- Unearthed electrical equipment. Dishwashers, driers, washing machines, and televisions are normally earthed. Special sockets are fitted to hobs, cookers and ovens.

- Timed earth trips. You sometimes have to wait several minutes after replacing a fuse before the normal supply is restored.

- Insecure light fittings and loose wall sockets.

- Imported electrical equipment not set for the French 220 volt/50 cycle system, or not fitted with a slow start system. The power surge produced by turning on an imported electric kettle or microwave is often sufficient to blow the fuses.

Useful words and phrases

Branch	Electrical connection (also brancher/branchment)
Disjonteur	The earth trip

Electricien	Electrician
Une fiche	A plug
Un fil	A wire (also un fil electrique)
Une fusable	A fuse
Une prise	A wall socket
Une traplice	An adapter

Gas

Gas in France is town gas or bottled gas. Town gas is mainly available in more densely populated urban areas and not at all in the countryside.

As electricity is relatively cheap, the visitor is often surprised to learn that most French homes have a back up (usually bottled) gas supply. There will often be a second (gas) hob fitted in the kitchen near to the electric one.

The reason is that electricity supplies are regularly interrupted. This is sometimes because of a generation or system failure, and sometimes as a result of industrial action.

Town gas suppliers offer a number of tariffs. UK property owners are sometimes confused by the French system of invoicing on the basis of kilowatt. This formula is based on the number of cubic metres of gas burnt to supply an equivalent number of kilowatts. As UK bills were changed from therms to kilowatt hours in 1992 confusion should not last long.

Where gas is only used for cooking in shared buildings, the bills are normally paid by the co-propriété and added to individual service charges.

Useful words and phrases

Une conduite	A pipe (also une conduite de gaz)
D'Urgence	The emergency service (also Depannage d'Urgence)
Une fuite	A gas leak (also une fuite de gaz)
Sapeurs Pompiers	The Fire Brigade (dial 18)

Water

All water is metered and bills are sent out by the local **Cie (Compagnie) des Eaux** (water company).

The metres are reliable and it is difficult to question charges. There are special rates for industrial and agricultural use, and for swimming pools.

Average annual water bills are around 60 per cent higher than in the UK. This fact, coupled with the psychological effect of metering, explains why in France you will rarely see a domestic sprinkler system or hosepipe in operation.

Telephones (PTT)

Applications for a telephone are made to the local **Agence Commerciale de Télécommunications**. Installations have been known to take place the following day but delays of up to 12 months are equally common.

Those used to the UK's standard installation system are sometimes shocked by charges levied in France. Connections within a block of flats are inexpensive, but if your new home is several miles from existing connections the charge will reflect the work involved.

The standard connection is called the **ligne mixte**. This is not a party line, but one that allows calls to be made in and out.

Points to note

- Ex-directory numbers are subject to a monthly surcharge.

- There are two phone books for each departement — the **annuaire** (domestic listings) and the professions *(Yellow Pages)*. The annuaire lists subscribers under towns and communes. The professions contains business listings and all those useful numbers that UK subscribers are used to finding in their standard phonebook.

- French phone numbers have eight digits arranged in four blocks of two. The first two digits are the area code. Dialling Paris is a special case. You dial 16 first, wait for a tone, dial 1 and follow it by the eight digit number.

- For international calls you dial 19, wait for the tone, then dial the country (the UK is 44), then the area code (omitting the first 0), and finally the local number.

- To reverse charges dial 10 and ask to make a PCV call. Give the operator the area and local codes and the name of the subscriber.

- There are three kinds of phone boxes in France. The **Taxi** box accepts only small coins and is limited to local calls. The **inter-urbain** box takes a wide range of coinage and can be used for long distance and international calls. The **télécarte** box is a card operated version of the inter-urbain. As in the UK the télécarte boxes are becoming most common. Cards can be bought at post offices, cafés and tabacs.

- Lines may go silent between phases of dialling a number, and the ringing tone is frequently inaudible.

Other useful numbers

Ambulance	Dial 17
Directory Enquiries	Dial 12
Engineers and Repairs	Dial 13
Fire Brigade	Dial 18
Police	Dial 17

Those used to the relative efficiency of BT may find its French equivalent — the PTT — a source of frustration. Lines, particularly into the capital, are overloaded and regularly unavailable during office hours.

PTT Directory Enquiries have a poor record of giving correct numbers. Checking overseas listings is often beyond them. If you are likely to contact the UK regularly it is worthwhile noting the number of a non automatic exchange, or even calling a friend to check the phone book for you.

Minitel

The flagship of automation in the PTT system is Minitel. This is a home based computer system which provides banks of useful data along the lines of teletext.

Minitel can also be used for access to bank accounts, sending telexes, and playing games. Television and radio phone-in programmes make use of Minitel, which can also be used to check share prices, road conditions, and railway and airline timetables.

Minitel is available free on request from your local agence commerciale des telecommunications.

THE MEDIA

The French media is generally more serious minded than in the UK. Nowhere is this more true than in television.

Television

There are six network channels in France with up to 24 hours broadcasting. Two channels are state controlled, and the others are monitored by an official watchdog organisation which has the power to revoke their licenses.

The formula is similar to the UK with a large number of quiz shows, sit-coms, movies and news programmes. The French do not quite share the British addiction to soaps, but they enjoy comedy and variety. There is a fair amount of arts programming and a great deal of political debate and discussion.

The French SECAM system is incompatible with the UK PAL standard. Conversions are possible but they are expensive. It is generally easier to buy a new set, unless you plan to rely entirely on satellite transmissions.

The ASTRA satellites already beam down almost 40 channels. France is at the heart of the 'footprint' and reception (even with a small 20 cm dish) is excellent. Eight channels carry free English language soundtrack programmes, and more (mainly film channels) are available on subscription. Three (German) high definition channels are already operational and English language broadcasting will begin using this wide screen NICAM format in the mid 1990s. To receive satellite programmes you need a dish and decoder.

Along parts of the northern coast and up to 20 miles inland it is possible to receive UK television signals. In sheltered positions a signal booster is required.

Radio

Radio reception is generally excellent in France.

The main stations are:

France-Culture	Concerned with the arts and literature.
France-Inter	Mainly current events and discussions.
France Musique	Mainly classical music and jazz.

There are dozens of FM commercial stations offering pop, easy listening, sport and news updates.

BBC for Europe (MW 648 khz/463 m) transmits around the clock with most daytime programmes in English. Radio 1, Radio 2, and Radio 5 can be picked up close to the northern coast. Radio 4 reception is adequate as far south as the Loire valley.

Newspapers

The most widely distributed newspapers are:

L'Equipe	Very successful daily paper. Emphasis on sport.
Le Figaro	Right of Centre quality daily.
France-Soir	Similar to UK tabloids in approach and content.
Le Monde	Independent left of centre quality daily.

English newspapers are widely distributed in France, especially during the holiday season. South of the channel ports and Paris you are most likely to see yesterday's newsprint on the stands.

A number of UK papers can appear in a modified (reduced) format. One of these is the *Continental Daily Mail*. Others, like the *Guardian Weekly*, are special editions prepared for the European market.

MOTORING

This is an area in which many potential residents already have a fair amount of knowledge. The following paragraphs outline the main requirements of law and the system of fixed penalty fines for those who break it.

The driver and the law

- You have to be over 18 with a full driving licence to drive in France.

- The French drive on the right.

- It is a legal requirement to carry a red warning triangle and a spare set of light bulbs.

- Third party insurance is compulsory.

- Driving documents, including your licence and vehicle registration document, must be available for inspection.

You are advised to carry a **constat** — a specially printed form to be filled in immediately after an accident. This can prevent difficulties with insurance claims, especially if there is hidden damage to your vehicle.

French roads are designated as motorways (A for autoroute), routes nationales (N roads) and routes departmentales (D roads). Most motorways are toll roads with a speed limit of 130 kph. 110 kph is the norm for dual carriageways, 90 kph for single carriageways, and 60 kph in urban areas. Routes nationales are frequently much less busy than their British equivalents.

Speed limits are rigorously enforced by traffic police. Toll cards are time stamped and there are both radar and camera speed traps. For minor offences (**contraventions**) police can impose a fixed penalty fine (**amende forfaitaire**).

This fixed penalty scheme includes:

- Not using seat belts, carrying a child under ten in the front seat, illegal use of the horn, and causing an obstruction — all 130 francs.

● Dangerous parking or parking at a bus stop, careless driving, ignoring signs and priority rules, speeding, and failing to stop at a traffic light — all 900 francs.

Failure to pay fixed penalty fines within 30 days means the offence is reclassified as **une amende majorée**. These are dealt with through the courts and fine levels are increased by 120 per cent.

The legal limit for drinking and driving is the same as in the UK. The law is applied in much the same way and penalties are equally severe.

The French penalty system is efficient, some would say ruthless. Despite this severity French driving behaviour, especially in busy towns, can create the impression that there is no law at all. Most French roads are quieter than those in the UK, but accident statistics in peak holiday periods make horrific reading.

If you bring a vehicle to France and stay less than six months you do not require a full customs declaration. You are however advised to obtain an international licence (essentially an extension and translation of the UK licence).

Driving licence

The British driving licence is valid in France for 12 months. If you are likely to be spending more time in France than the UK it is recommended that you apply for a French licence as soon as you receive your resident's permit. Remember you are not entitled to hold 'dual nationality of the road'. The UK licence must be surrendered with the application for the French one.

If you do not exchange licences within twelve months you will have to take the French driving test which is altogether more rigorous than its UK counterpart.

The French issuing authority is the **Service du Permis de Conduire de la Préfecture de Police**.

Importing a vehicle

If you import your vehicle you will require French licence plates (**plaques d'immatriculation**) after six months.

You apply to the préfecture de police who send you a number which a local garage will make up and fit for a modest fee.

Vehicle owners are also required to obtain registration documents for the vehicle (the **carte grise**). A **carnet de passage en douanes** (certificate of passage through customs) is a further vital document to retain, especially if you are considering importing the vehicle.

Duty

French residents (and temporary residents) who import their vehicles from the UK within 12 months can do so tax free.

There is no limit on the number of vehicles that can be imported. The rule is they must have been the personal property of the resident for six months prior to import and they cannot be sold for six months after the import date.

If you intend to import a vehicle you will require documentation from a French consulate in the UK.

Buying a vehicle in France

There are advantages to this:

● Vehicle values are lower in France despite the UK's reduction of the rate of special vehicle tax in 1992.

● For up to six months you can run the vehicle on temporary (TT) plates if you pay in foreign currency.

● Left hand drive vehicles are safer to drive and easier to sell. There are some small, but significant parts for RHD vehicles that are difficult, or impossible to obtain in France. Accelerator cables, for instance, are invariably a different length.

Insurance

In the short term you can extend your UK cover by asking your insurers for an international insurance certificate (green card). This means you will pay a supplementary premium. Motor insurance for unlimited third-party liability is compulsory in France. Premiums are relatively expensive and the services of a good broker are recommended.

The **Centre de Documentation et d'Information sur les Assurances**, 2 Rue Chaussée d'Antin, 75009 Paris, Tel (1) 48.24.96.12, provides lists of recognised and approved brokers in each region.

The following organisations can offer more complete advice about this, and other matters relating to import, licensing, and registration:

Automobile Club d'Ile de France
8 place de la Concorde
75008 Paris.
Tel: (1) 42.66.43.00.

Touring Club de France
14 avenue de la Grande Armée
75017 Paris.
Tel: (1) 43.80.68.58.

La Vignette (road tax)

The French system of road tax is unusual and for some it can prove to be a major item of expenditure. What you pay depends on the age of the vehicle, its power, and where you live. When you pay the tax you are issued with a certificate.

Vehicles are classed as:

● Less than 5 years old. Between 5 and 20 years old. More than 20 years old.

● In nine categories from less than 5 CV to 23 CV and above.

● Belonging to a particular département. The cost of road repairs in that département is taken into consideration.

The following abbreviated table may be a useful guide. Prices are approximate and given in pounds (and assumes 10 francs = 1 pound):

	Less than five years old				
	U5CV	5-7CV	10-11CV	19-20CV	23CV+
Paris	19	36	102	406	917
Corsica	13	24	67	268	605
Haute Provence	25	48	133	527	1190

Fig. 7. Road tax guide for newer cars.

Vehicles more than five but less than 20 years old					
	U5CV	5-7CV	10-11CV	19-20CV	23CV+
Paris	10	18	51	203	456
Corsica	6	12	34	134	302
Haute Provence	12	24	66	263	595

Vehicles more than 20 years old pay a nominal vignette, normally less than £10. (Figures: Macdonald Research, 1991.)

Fig. 8. Road tax guide for older cars.

A few small cars, such as the Fiat Panda, will fit within the lowest — under 5 CV — category. Most family cars will fit into the 5-7CV category. High performance cars, such as the BMW series 7 will be in between the 10-11CV and 19-20CV categories. Only the owners of top of the range Porsches, Ferraris and similar prestige vehicles will fit into the highest categories.

The vignette is considered to be a much fairer system than UK road tax. It combines freedom of choice with ability to pay and environmental concerns. In France all the money is actually spent on the roads.

There are hefty fines for those who do not display a valid vignette on their windscreen. UK drivers are normally exempt until the expiry of their UK tax certificate, though technically it is an offence to run a car with old plates within a new département for more than three months. The general rule is that once a car has French plates it must display a valid certificate.

Service de Mines
This is similar to the UK MOT and is a general roadworthiness test.

The demands for testing are sent out by départements at different times of the year. For cars imported from the UK headlights will have to be realigned for the right hand side of the road and fitted with yellow bulbs.

Passing the roadworthiness test secures you the **carte grise** — a document that must be produced when your insurance is renewed.

5
Financial Matters

BANKING IN FRANCE

Though it is theoretically possible for residents to manage without a French bank account, it is undoubtedly more convenient to have one. French banking rules are, however, rather different to those in most other EC countries. It is best to be aware of the way the system works.

The differences
Exchange controls were lifted in the UK some years ago which means you can take an unlimited amount of sterling into France. You are however only permitted to take 50,000 francs out of the country at any one time. The situation is likely to change at any time, and the Banque de France has generally made an exception for foreigners who wish to export the net proceeds of a property sale.

Opening a bank account
Foreigners can open a special account called a **compte étranger** literally a stranger's account. Sterling can be paid in by normal bank transfer methods, or by cheque or cash. The French government has sought to reduce tax evasion by discouraging 'cash' deals. This means that French notes and coinage cannot be paid into bank accounts.

The compte étranger can be an ordinary/current account **compte cheques** or a deposit account **compte sur livret**. The ordinary account provides you with a chequebook, and the deposit account pays interest. Orders for new chequebooks can take several weeks to process so it is best to keep a spare book.

Arrangements for statements are similar to those in force in the UK, but it is unwise to assume that your statement is up to date. There are good reasons why the French clearing system is referred to as la tortue — the tortoise. . .

When you open an account the bank will check with central records to find out if you are subject to an interdiction — a ban from holding a bank account. Inter-bank communication is excellent. A UK bankruptcy, a withdrawal of credit notice, or a court order for debt or non payment, will almost certainly prevent you from opening an ordinary account.

Interest

Gross interest is paid on deposit accounts. It is your responsibility to declare this to the taxman either in France or the UK. The double taxation agreement between the countries means that you are only liable to pay tax once.

Most banks impose a minimum balance for ordinary accounts — usually around 500 francs. Interest is not ordinarily paid on these accounts unless you agree to maintain a higher minimum balance.

Credits and debits

Cheques paid into your account are credited on the same day, even if post-dated, but you cannot draw against them until clearance is complete.

French cheques are similar to the UK model with the amount written in both words and numbers. If the amounts are different the words will be assumed to be correct. Cheques must be endorsed. Open cheques will be honoured but this can lead to delay. Crossed cheques are recommended. Cheques can only be stopped for security reasons — this generally means notifying the bank that it has been lost or stolen.

Using — and misusing — your cheques

French law allows traders to refuse a cheque for any amount less than 10,000 francs, and cash for any amount greater than that. Both events are now rare. Indeed, as part of the continued battle against 'cash' deals, French law now insists that cheques are issued as payment for work or services valued at more than 1,000 francs. The law has recently been extended to apply to rents and office supplies.

Cheque guarantee cards are not issued in France, but some form of proof of identity is likely to be required. French nationals carry identity cards.

The French are very tough on misuse of bank accounts. If you bounce a cheque the bank will instruct you to put matters right. If you fail to do so within the 30 day time limit your cheque book will be withdrawn, the account is frozen and you are subject to a ban (an **interdiction**). The ban is recorded with the Banque de France and the file is retained for two years during which time you may not open or operate a bank account in France. Even if your account is regularised within 30 days, a second offence within the year will incur a 12 month chequebook ban.

Financial penalties for bouncing cheques are severe. These can range from a fine of 3,000 to 250,000 francs. Prison sentences of up to five years can be (and occasionally are) imposed. Misunderstanding the system, or claiming the problem arose through the slowness of the clearing system have not proved to be adequate defences in law.

UK banks in France

All the major UK banks are represented in France, although outside the major cities the branches are thinly distributed.

The advantage of dealing with a UK bank in France is primarily one of communication. Banks of all nationalities are subject to French banking law.

Bank dispensers

Bank cash dispensers (**distributeurs**) are similar to those operating in the UK, with the additional advantage that many offer an English language program for transactions.

For a modest fee French banks will issue a **carte de retrait** (withdrawal card). Much better, but pricier, is a **carte de paiement national** which allows withdrawals from any dispenser in the Carte Bancaire group which includes most of the major banks. Carte Bancaire dispensers are identified by the distinctive CB logo.

Dispensers can be found on high streets and at strategic points close to hypermarkets and shopping precincts.

Credit cards

The use of **le plastique** is now commonplace in France.

The Visa card is by far the most useful, as Visa is part of the Carte Bancaire group, but a larger number of points of sale are now accepting Mastercard. UK pins are accepted by most dispensers for cash withdrawals. Statements can be sent directly from the UK.

Some French traders (particularly supermarkets) will not accept credit cards or cheques for small amounts — usually less than 100 francs. Traders must have a clear sign showing that this policy is in force.

American Express is accepted in up-market hotels, restaurants and stores. These are mainly found in the capital and larger towns and cities.

Emergencies

Loss of UK Visa card

Contact Barclaycard Headquarters in Northampton. Tel: +19 44 604 230

230. Notify the bank branch that issued the card. A replacement card can be issued immediately.

Loss of UK Mastercard
Contact Access Headquarters in Southend, Essex. Tel: +19 44 702, then 362 988 for Lloyds Bank, 352 244 for Midland Bank, or 352 255 for National Westminster Bank. A new card can be issued immediately.

Loss of UK cheque books and cash cards
Notify your branch immediately and give them as much information as possible about outstanding cheques. If theft is suspected the bank will temporarily freeze your account.

Loss of French cheque books and cards
Telephone your branch straight away. Tell them what has happened. They will temporarily freeze the account and you should confirm your instructions in writing. French banks are responsible for losses only after they have been notified.

Theft
UK and French banks will always make special arrangements to help following the theft of cash, cheque books and credit cards. A credit line or cash withdrawal facility can normally be arranged within 24 hours. At weekends you may need to contact a consulate or the financial counsellor of the British Embassy in Paris. Tel: (1) 42.66.91.42.

TAXATION

The French levy tax at both national and local level. UK nationals may normally opt to pay income tax in either country.

Personal taxation
The basic taxes for individuals are:

● Income tax. This is divided in French law into earned income (**impôt sur le revenue** and unearned income (**impôt des revenues des capitaux mobiliers**).

● Land tax (**taxe foncière**).

● Community tax (**taxe d'habitation**).

- Capital gains tax (**régime des plus-values des particuliers**).

- Death duties (**droits de succession**).

- Gift tax (**droits de donation**).

Registration

The ownership of all properties must be registered with the French tax authorities. Owners who are not resident have to register by 30th April following completion of the property purchase. Residents are expected to register immediately with the local Centre des Impôts. Non resident owners should register with the Tax Centre for Non Residents at:

Centre des Impôts des Non-résidents
9 rue D'Uzes
75084 Paris.

Domicile

For international tax purposes the concept of domicile is important. Those who have their **fiscal domicile** in France pay tax there on all their income. Those considered to be domiciled elsewhere pay tax only on that portion of their income earned in France.

You will be said to have a French fiscal domicile if:

- You have a home in France and spend more than 183 days in the country in any financial year.

- Your wife and family live in France for more than 183 days in any financial year, even if you spend most of your time out of the country.

- You work in France on either a salaried or self employed basis, unless you can prove that work is ancillary to your main employment.

- Most of your income is generated in France. This could for instance catch retired people who run a successful gîte business.

Income tax

If you are domiciled in France you are liable to pay income tax. The French tax laws are complex and there will be winners and losers in comparison with the UK system.

Long term residents frequently choose to take French citizenship because foreigners are subject to an increasingly heavy burden of personal taxation.

There is an outline of the system below. Detailed information is available from a French government interdepartmental economic agency — Delegation à L'Amènagement du Territoire et à L'Action Regionale (**DATAR**). Their UK address is:

21-24 Grosvenor Place
London SW1X 7HU.
Tel: (071) 235 5140.

Essentially DATAR's UK office is intended to offer fiscal advice for anyone considering selling to the French market, or setting up a business in France itself. Their publications include helpful advice on personal taxation.

French income tax is assessed on a family basis. The husband is responsible for the return which includes the income of his wife and children who are still in the educational system, or doing their military service. Divorced, separated or widowed persons claim allowances according to circumstances.

Tax allowances
Across the board allowances include:

● Money spent on major property repairs.

● Money spent on certain 'green projects' such as the installation of solar energy panels for heating.

● Payments for maintenance and dependent relatives other than children.

● Gifts to certain charities.

● Contributions to the Securité Sociale.

● Approved life assurance premiums.

● Interest payments on certain loans.

● Special arrangements for single parents with young children.

Calculating taxable income

Taxable income is worked out by deducting allowances from total income and dividing the net figure by:

● 1.0 for a single person with no children.

● 2.0 for a married couple with no children.

● 2.5 for a married couple with one child.

● An extra 0.5 for each additional child. A married couple with four children will divide by four.

When a taxable income has been worked out the rates that apply fall into a banded structure. The following are approximate figures for those incurring an income tax liability in France in 1992. They are based on indexing the tax authorities' 1991 figures and converting them to sterling equivalents at an assumed rate of exchange of ten francs to the pound. The following bands should be treated only as a rough guide:

The first £3,400 of taxable income is tax free.

£3,401 to £3,700	five per cent
£3,701 to £4,200	ten per cent
£4,201 to £6,500	15 per cent
£6,501 to £8,400	20 per cent
£8,401 to £11,000	25 per cent
£11,001 to £12,800	30 per cent
£12,801 to £15,200	35 per cent
£15,201 to £24,600	40 per cent
£24,601 to £34,800	45 per cent
£34,801 to £40,300	50 per cent
£40,301 to £46,400	55 per cent
£46,001 and upwards	58 per cent

A married couple with no children, no allowances and a joint income of £25,000 would pay tax as follows:

Half of £25,000 is £12,500, so each has a taxable income of £12,500.

On the first £3,400 no tax is paid

On the next £300	at 5 per cent	£15
On the next £500	at 10 per cent	£50
On the next £2,300	at 15 per cent	£345
On the next £1,900	at 20 per cent	£380
On the next £2,600	at 25 per cent	£650
On the final £1,500	at 30 per cent	£500
Total		£1,940

Thus their joint tax bill would be (£1,940 x 2) £3,880.

The same couple living in England would automatically have personal allowances of £3,295 each and in addition, one of them, usually the man, would have a married person's allowance of £1,720. Their tax bill would look like this:

Woman's taxable income £12,500 - £3,295	= £9,205
Tax on £9,205 at 25 per cent	= £2,301.25
Man's taxable income £12,500 - £3,295 - £1,720	= £7,485
Tax on £7,485 at 25 per cent	= £1,871.25
Total tax bill £2,301 + £1,871.25	= £4,172.25

Thus their joint tax bill would be (£2,301.25 + £1,871.25) £4,172.25.

The French tax system benefits large families and those on relatively low incomes. The tax year runs from January 1st each year and bills are paid in three equal instalments in the year following the liability.

Filling in a tax return is difficult because of the complexity of the system and the amount of technical language involved. English speaking residents paying income tax in France invariably require the services of an accountant.

When the authorities suspect that tax declarations are inaccurate or fraudulent they will investigate. In certain circumstances residents with complex tax affairs (including perhaps income from a number of sources outside France) will be assessed according to the punitive **régime de l'imposition forfaiture**.

Using this system income is assessed according to arbitrary norms. This includes ascribing a letting value to all properties you own and multiplying it by a factor of three or five. Cars are valued and taxed at 75 per cent of maximum new showroom value, servants are assumed to have massive salaries, and race horses are reckoned to be winners.

The system is rarely applied but it demonstrates what can happen to those who fall foul of the tax authorities.

Land tax

Taxe foncière is levied by the local commune and is very similar to the system of parish rates in the UK. Registers of all property and owners are maintained at the mairie.

Property is given a notional letting value on which the taxe foncière is based. Exceptions include government and public buildings, grain stores, wine presses and stables. New buildings are exempt from the tax for two years.

The last general valuation of buildings was carried out in 1974. The tax levied is adjusted annually in line with the index of inflation.

Community tax

Taxe d'habitation is paid by the resident occupier of a property on January 1st each year. It is calculated according to the value of amenities. These include the size of the property, including garages, outbuildings and land. If the property is not subject to a lease, then the owner of the property is liable for the payment of the tax.

The base rate of the tax is calculated again on the notional letting value of the property, last calculated in 1987 and uprated since then by approximately 5 per cent.

This tax is reduced when the property is used as the principal residence of a family. Since 1989 each commune has fixed taxe d'habitation at rates of five, ten or 15 per cent of the lettable value.

Both taxe foncière and taxe d'habitation are payable by UK residents whether or not the property is designated as their main residence.

Capital Gains Tax

The **régime de plus value des particuliers** is imposed on anyone who is domiciled in France when assets are sold, but their primary residence is exempted. It is generally applied to residents (domiciled elsewhere) who sell any property in France.

The tax is levied at 33 per cent. The capital gain is deemed to be the difference between purchase price and sale price, but the seller can offset:

- The supplementary costs of making the purchase, or ten per cent of the purchase price — whichever is the higher figure.

- An indexation of the increase in property values calculated according to government figures.

French law demands that foreign sellers employ an agent to handle the sale. This agent (normally a **notaire**) is responsible for paying the tax to the government. It is possible to get clearance for payment before completion. This is highly recommended. It saves time and paperwork and will reduce the fee the agent charges for his services.

In practice the capital gains tax payable on a property sale is likely to be modest or non existent for many sellers. Those who improve property considerably, or create new residential units (such as a granny flat) are most likely to find themselves paying for the privilege.

Inheritance Tax
French law is very concerned with the idea of passing down assets within a family. The concept is called **patrimoine** and it is the guiding principle of **droits de succession**.

This is subject to the following rules:

- Payments are made by those who inherit, according to the value of assets they receive and their relationship to the deceased.

- All assets in France are subject to droits de succession.

- The assets of those domiciled in France include property at home and abroad.

- The assets of those not domiciled in France exclude property outside the country. Double tax agreements with other countries ensure that droits de succession paid in France are exempted from tax liability elsewhere.

Inheritance Tax rates
The rates of inheritance tax given below are based on current bands. Figures have again been converted in sterling and assume 10 francs to the pound.

When an estate passes to a surviving spouse or a relative in direct ascendant or descendant line there is a tax free allowance of £27,000 per beneficiary.

After that a surviving spouse pays:

Five per cent on the next £5,000

10 per cent on amounts between £5,000 and £10,000

15 per cent on amounts between £10,000 and £20,000

20 per cent on amounts between £20,000 and £340,000

30 per cent on amounts between £340,000 and £560,000

35 per cent on amounts between £560,000 and £1,200,000

40 per cent on amounts in excess of £1,200,000.

The ascendant or descendant relative pays:

5 per cent on the next £5,000

10 per cent on amounts between £5,000 and £7,500

15 per cent on amounts between £7,500 and £10,000

20 per cent on amounts between £10,000 and £340,000

25 per cent on amounts between £340,000 and £560,000

30 per cent on amounts between £560,000 and £1,200,000

40 per cent on amounts in excess of £1,200,000.

Divorced or unmarried brothers and sisters have a beneficiary allowance of £10,000. The same allowance can be claimed if they are more than 50 years of age or suffer from infirmity. After this they pay:

35 per cent on all amounts up to £15,000

45 per cent on all amounts above £15,000.

Third degree relatives — aunts, uncles, nephews, nieces and cousins pay 55 per cent of the inheritance received.

Any other beneficiary (apart from certain charities) will pay a rate of 60 per cent.

Gift Tax

The rules for **droits de donation** are similar to those applied above. The idea is to prevent the avoidance of inheritance tax.

There is some mitigation for:

● Gifts given as wedding presents.

● Gifts made by people under the age of 65.

Wealth Tax
No longer exists in France.

Value Added Tax
There are presently four rates of **Taxe sur la valeur ajoutée** (TVA) in France:

● 5.5 per cent for most agricultural and food products.

● 7 per cent on travel, entertainment, catering, hotels, medicines and most books.

● A standard rate of 18.6 per cent for most other items.

● 33 per cent on luxury goods, tobacco, and pornography. The French call this **taxe de pêche** — sin tax.

The sale of new properties (or any first sale within five years of construction) is subject to TVA. This will always be included in the sale price and will be paid by the developer.

Any property re-sold within that five year period is also subject to TVA. This concerns UK buyers more than is necessary. The amount is not usually considerable because the seller offsets the amount paid in TVA on the initial sale, and French property values have advanced more cautiously than our own. Only when a property has been substantially improved or modified during the five year period is it likely to attract a significant TVA bill.

WILLS AND INHERITANCE

Le testament is an important document for all those considering entering the French property market.

When you own French property the rules concerning its disposition are French. Even if a dispute about ownership or inheritance originates in the UK the law that will decide the outcome will be French.

Livret de famille

Under French law every family is required to keep a **livret de famille** (family booklet). A marriage opens a new livret and details of births, adoptions and deaths are added. When a couple divorce two separate copies are created and when a death occurs the livret is handed in.

It is an offence not to keep the livret up to date. Although the French issue certificates for births, marriages and deaths, it is the livret that provides the onus of proof in the law of inheritance.

Non French residents are not required to maintain this document. However, the livret demonstrates two things:

1. The French are keen on written evidence. Proving a will in France may prove difficult without a full set of family certificates, affidavits, and decrees.

2. There are important precedents in French civil law about the status of the family and the members of the family group. This begins to explain why rules of succession are more important than the wishes of the individual in matters of inheritance.

Rules of succession

The French are required by law to leave most of their estate to their family. Residents' assets are dealt with under the rules of domicile, but these do not include property which is always passed on according to French laws of succession.

Precedence is given to ascendant and descendant heirs — the **héritiers réservée**. The inheritance rules are:

●   One child will inherit at least half the estate.

●   Two children between them will inherit at least two thirds of the estate.

●   Three or more children will share at least three quarters of the estate.

●   The surviving spouse (who is not a heritier reservée) will inherit half, a third, or a quarter of the estate, or a life interest in the estate which will pass to the children on his or her death.

●   The remaining portion of the estate is freely disposable (**quotité disponible**). If there are no surviving ascendants, descendants, or spouse, the whole estate would become freely disposable.

● The surviving spouse is entitled to continue to enjoy the marital property during his or her lifetime.

Residents have made various attempts to get round the rules of succession. One of these is to set up trusts but they have not been recognised in French courts.

Co-ownership

There is one legal way to offset some of the impact of the inheritance rules. This is to arrange the property purchase as a co-ownership with a contract clause that allows the surviving partner to inherit. The survivor could then choose:

● to sell the property and take the net proceeds beyond the rule of French law;

● to stay in the property as sole owner. If this happens the estate of the survivor will become subject to the normal rules of domicile and succession.

A French lawyer can draw up a contract of co-ownership, although he would be surprised if he was asked to perform this service for a married couple.

En Tontine

The French would do this rather differently through an arrangement called **en tontine**. This was originally intended to avoid the break up of large (generally agricultural) estates. Those who would ordinarily have rights under the rules of succession are bypassed in favour of the surviving owner, or the last surviving héritier reservée.

Neither en tontine or co-ownership help to avoid death duties, but they may help to ensure that the property is disposed of according to your wishes.

The will as a document

Three kinds of will are provable under French law.

The testament olographe

This is handwritten, signed and dated by the testator. Any written addition, including the signature of a witness invalidates it.

The testament authentique
This is dictated by the testator and witnessed by two notaires, or one notaire and two adult witnesses.

The testament mystique
This is a handwritten or typescript document signed by the testator and sealed in an envelope in the presence of two witnesses. The witnesses then hand the envelope to a notaire who signs the sealed envelope himself. He dates it, notes the names of the witnesses, and adds a written declaration that he understands the envelope to contain the will of a named testator.

Validation of wills
Rules for validating wills in France are very strict. The more complex the document and the greater the number of witnesses, the more likely it is to become void.

The rules for proving a will in the UK are as different as the kind of document that is acceptable. Rules of intestacy are also different. In France the whole of the property would be divided according to laws of succession that favour children. In the UK the law favours the surviving spouse. It is also worth noting that in France marriage does not automatically revoke an existing will.

Intestacy profits nobody but the lawyers, and this is doubly true for double intestacy. The importance of taking good advice when property and assets are held in more than one country cannot be over stressed.

Executors

Under UK law an executor is technically the owner of the testator's assets and property. He discharges the responsibility of ownership by paying debts and duties and distributing the residue estate in accordance with the testator's wishes as indicated in the will.

In France the position is different. Property is deemed to pass directly to heirs under the rules of succession and an executor is not necessary. Debts and duties are the responsibility of the heirs, but an **exécuteur testamentaire** may be appointed to help supervise other aspects of the process of inheritance.

This service is important if specific items of furniture and jewellery are intended to pass to named beneficiaries within that part of the estate which is freely disposable (quotité disponible). A notaire can be appointed to carry out this service (for a fee), but any adult can be asked by the testator to accept the responsibility. The executeur testamentaire must be named in the will and should not be one of the major beneficiaries.

MORTGAGES AND LOANS

When considering mortgage options the UK borrower begins with two basic choices:

1. Borrowing in the UK against a UK security — normally a new or second mortgage on a property.

2. Borrowing in France against the security of the property purchased.

It is generally accepted that if you have to borrow it should either be in the currency of your income or in the currency of the country where you are buying the property.

Raising finance in the UK

Banks and building societies have competed fiercely for mortgage business in recent years. The situation could change rapidly if credit controls are introduced, or if money supply is limited in some other way. If this happens mortgage applications for second homes in particular are unlikely to be regarded with much favour.

It should also be noted:

● A first mortgage secured against a UK property is eligible for tax relief up to £30,000.

● A mortgage can be secured against assets other than property.

● A bank or building society who hold a first mortgage on a UK property may be willing to extend the mortgage facility with the minimum of formalities if the account has been properly conducted.

● Borrowers who have paid mortgages on the same property during the boom period of the 1980s may well have considerable equity in that property. Banks are usually prepared to lend up to 80 per cent of the total equity value when an additional amount is requested to invest in foreign property.

● Any new mortgage or loan is likely to be subject to legal and arrangement fees.

● Raising money in the UK may be easier in terms of communication.

● When finance is raised in advance in the UK and deposited in a French bank, you are effectively offering a cash transaction. This can be advantageous in negotiating a reduction in the asking price.

Foreign currency loans

It may also be possible to raise a foreign currency loan secured against UK property. One advantage of this is that the loan can be fixed for a repayment period much shorter than a mortgage. Another advantage is that capital is repaid alongside interest even at the early stages of repayment, something which happens to a much smaller degree with mortgages.

A loan is charged at a higher interest rate than a mortgage, but because the repayment period is much shorter it is likely to prove to be a less expensive option. A loan may be of particular benefit to people approaching retirement age.

One problem with a foreign currency loan is what can happen if the borrower is unable to maintain repayments. If the bank sells the secured property there may well be a surplus in sterling terms which could become a shortfall when converted into foreign currency.

When negotiating loans banks may ask for insurance cover against default in repayments. This cover is to protect the lending institution, not the borrower, and in the event of a claim is paid directly to them.

Endowment mortgages

Borrowers are also likely to be offered loans which include endowments and pension plans. Tied packages of this kind may be more in the interest of the lender than the borrower, who frequently benefits most from a simple repayment scheme.

Before signing any loan or mortgage agreement potential borrowers are urged to seek independent financial advice.

Raising finance in France

Many financial institutions in France offer loans, but it is mainly the banks that provide long term (mortgage) finance.

Here are some important features of a French loan.

Interest rates

Interest rates in France are historically lower than those in the UK and attractive Government subsidies can apply to the purchase of a main residence. These loans are difficult, but not impossible, to obtain. However, if you accept a subsidy loan, you undertake to live in the premises for eight months a year. This in turn means you become legally domiciled in France.

Interest rates are generally fixed for the whole term of the mortgage. Around 11 per cent has been typical in recent years.

Reversible rate mortgages are negotiable. This means that the interest rate is fixed for a period and then revised within certain boundaries. When interest rates are high this can be a good option.

Arrangement fees
French financial institutions charge around one per cent of the loan as an arrangement fee.

Special savings loans
Some borrowers may be eligible for a special savings (**épargne logement**) loan. These are below normal rates and do not require the purchaser to become domiciled in France.

Currency of loans
Loans can be negotiated in a number of different currencies. The US dollar, Swiss franc, and German mark have all been seen at one time or another as advantageous to the borrower. This is partly speculative, and partly created by a market perception that some currencies are more stable than others.

Security
Security on the property will be required for all loans which will never be for more than 80 per cent of the purchase price. Premiums for life, health and disablement insurance are included in monthly repayments.

The banks
You will not be sold endowment or pension mortgage packages by French banks. These do not exist in France.

Cooling off periods
The law provides a 'cooling off' period (minimum ten days) after a formal loan offer has been received.

Comparisons
When checking current repayment rates of UK and French mortgages it is important to compare like with like. Take into account the term of years

offered (normally shorter in France) and add in insurances, arrangement and legal fees. UK financial institutions are coy about revealing the rates of commission they earn for setting up certain types of loans and mortgages, but sometimes these can add hundreds of pounds a year to your payments.

The following major French institutions are enthusiastic enough about UK mortgage business to have opened offices on this side of the channel. They also provide brochures and free information:

Banque Transatlantique
103 Mount St
London W1Y 5HE.
Tel: (071) 493 6717.

CIC Group
74 London Wall
London EC2M 5NE.
Tel: (071) 638 5700.

Crédit Agricole
23 Sheen Rd
Richmond
Surrey TW9 1BN.
Tel: (081) 332 0130.

Crédit Lyonnais
84-95 Queen Victoria Street
London EC4P 4LX.
Tel: (071) 634 8000.

Crédit du Nord
66 Mark Lane
London EC3R 7HS.
Tel: (071) 488 0872.

In addition to the major banking organisations loans can be negotiated through savings banks (**caisses d'épargne**) and notaires. All loans are subject to your financial status but the general rule is that your mortgage repayments and normal outgoings should not add up to more than 30 per cent of your gross income.

INSURANCE

Insurance requirements in France are different to the UK. The law demands that every property is covered by third party insurance (civil propriété). If your property is to be built the premium must be paid before work on the site begins.

French mortgage lenders (unlike their UK equivalents) do not insist that you take out buildings insurance. However it is strongly recommended that you do. This can be arranged separately or included in a comprehensive (**multirisque**) policy that also covers your possessions. UK insurers generally offer the most complete and competitive policies.

If you live in a block of flats the civil propriété and buildings policies will be paid communally. Check your lease or the terms of the sale agreement. In communal (co-owned) property you should always have adequate cover for your possessions.

If you let out your property, or allow someone to live in it, the tenant should indemnify you against the risk of fire. He is also responsible for insuring his own possessions.

6
The Purchase Process

It is possible to purchase a French property through a lawyer (a notaire) or even directly from the vendor. More than 50 per cent of properties, however, are bought through estate agencies.

THE ESTATE AGENT

The agent immobilier is much more respected in France than the UK. This may be partly because the profession is highly regulated. Before he can set up in business, he has to have:

- Standards of qualification, competence, and experience.

- A professional permit to cover all property transactions. The permit has to be revalidated annually by the local Préfecture de Police.

- Professional indemnity insurance.

- Bank guarantees that cover him for all money he holds on behalf of clients. It is illegal for him to hold any money if the guarantee is for less than £50,000.

- Up to date knowledge of the true cost of transactions and market values. He is required by law to give this information and to give it honestly.

- Power of attorney (**mandat de vente**) before he can negotiate any sale on behalf of the vendor. The mandat has to be renewed after three months. He cannot purchase any property himself for which he holds a mandat for sale.

- Specified rates of commission written into the power of attorney and prominently displayed in his office.

The FNAIM

The **Fédération Nationale des Agents Immobiliers** is the recognised trade association of estate agents. It operates at national, departmental, and local level providing data banks of agencies and properties for sale.

FNAIM information is available through MINITEL or through associate members. The national address is:

FNAIM
129 Rue de Faubourg St Honoré
75008 Paris.
Tel: (1) 42.25.24.26.

Payments to agents

In France the purchaser, rather than the vendor, often has to pay the agents commission. This is no longer universally so. Agents in some regions have now adopted the more common EC practice of charging the vendor.

It makes little difference in the end. The commission is usually hidden in the purchase price if the vendor pays it, or a property may seem unusually cheap if commission is to be added. Commission rates were fixed by law until 1987 but agents can now charge whatever they think the market can stand. In practice they usually ask 5 per cent (plus TVA at 18.6 per cent) but the rate can be higher for up-market properties. Sometimes a sliding scale is used.

The phrases to look out for are:

Commission comprise — commission included.
Commission non comprise — commission not included.

No commission is payable until the sale is legally finalised by the writing and recording of the deed.

THE NOTAIRE

The French solicitor, the **notaire**, is a highly qualified and respected individual:

● His authority is necessary to create valid contracts.

● His occupation is strictly regulated by the Ministry of Justice and his professional association the Chambre de Notaires.

- He is entitled to act (and usually does) for both parties in a property sale.

- He is obliged to impartially explain the implications of the clauses of contract.

- He is entitled to act as sales negotiator — taking on the role of the agent immobilier — for which he receives commission.

- He is invariably employed to negotiate complex sales such as those that involve co-ownership, or after death or divorce.

- He draws up the authentic act of sale, verifies the vendor's right to sell, checks planning regulations, and notes existing charges against the property. Where these are greater than the sale price he must be sure that the creditors can be paid in some other way.

- He is responsible for collecting registration fees and passing them on to the proper authorities.

Preliminary contracts

A contract for the sale of property in France is more like the Scottish system than the English. Once a preliminary contract has been signed it is difficult and expensive to back out of the deal. One advantage of the system is that gazumping is almost unknown in France.

There are two forms of contract in current use, the **compromis de vente** and the **promesse de vente**.

Compromis de vente

Signing the compromis de vente — literally compromise or implication of sale — means that vendor and purchaser are committed. It is possible to include 'get out' clauses in the contract (**conditions suspensives**) but these usually relate to obtaining a mortgage, checking the authority to sell and town planning reports.

Conditions suspensives take precedence over other contract clauses. If they cannot be fulfilled the contract becomes void and deposits are returned.

The compromis de vente is the normal form of agreement in a private sale. The contract can include agreed penalty clauses to be imposed on either vendor or purchaser if the sale breaks down for any reason other than those listed in the conditions suspensives.

The contract is usually a standard one (see fig. 9).

Vente
de biens et droits
immobiliers
sous conditions
suspensives

En présence et avec le concours de (1) . . . .

. . . .

représentant (2)

dénommé ci-après <LE REDACTEUR> des
présentes.

ENTRE LES SOUSSIGNES

M . . . .

. . . .

. . . .

. . . .

. . . .

. . . .

. . . .

intervenant aux présentes sous la dénomination «LE VENDEUR», d'une part ;

et M . . . .

. . . .

. . . .

. . . .

. . . .

. . . .

. . . .

Intervenant aux présentes sous la dénomination «L'ACQUEREUR», d'autre part ;

Etant précisé que si la vente intervient entre plusieurs vendeurs ou acquéreurs, les uns et les autres agiront conjointement et solidairement entre eux et seront dénommés dans la présente «LE VENDEUR» et «L'ACQUEREUR» au singulier.

Fig. 9. Contract of Sale — Compromis de Vente.

1 - Engagement

LE VENDEUR, en s'obligeant et en obligeant ses héritiers et ayants droit solidairement entre eux, fussentils mineurs ou incapables, à toutes les garanties ordinaires et de droit les plus étendues, VEND à l'ACQUEREUR qui accepte et S'ENGAGE A ACQUERIR , SOUS RESERVE DES CONDITIONS SUSPENSIVES ENONCEES AUX PRESENTES, les biens et droits immobiliers dont la désignation suit.

SITUATION ET DESIGNATION (3)

....

....

....

....

....

....

....

....

....

....

....

....

....

....

Tels que lesdits biens existent et se comportent dans leur état actuel, avec toutes leurs dépendances, sans aucune exception ni réserve, l'ACQUEREUR déclarant au surplus les bien connaître pour les avoir vus et visités et dispensant LE VENDEUR d'une plus ample désignation.

Fig. 9. Contract of Sale — Compromis de Vente (continued).

DECLARATIONS DU VENDEUR

Le VENDEUR déclare :

1° SUR L'ETAT CIVIL : Qu'il s'oblige à faire dans l'acte de réalisation des présentes les déclarations civiles d'usage et que rien dans ces déclarations ne s'oppose à cette réalisation.

2° SUR L'ORIGINE DE PROPRIETE : Qu'il est seul propriétaire des biens pour les avoir acquis

de M ....

par acte .... et qu'il s'engage à fournir à première demande du REDACTEUR des présentes et du NOTAIRE rédacteur de l'acte authentique, tous titres de propriété et pièces nécessaires à la vente.

3° SUR LES SERVITUDES ET L'URBANISME : Que les biens, object des présentes, ne sont à sa connaissance grevés d'aucune servitude autres que celles résultant de la situation naturelle des lieux, du plan d'aménagement et d'urbanisme et de la loi en général, les questions d'urbanisme faisant ci-après l'objet d'une condition suspensive.

4° SUR LA SITUATION HYPOTHECAIRE : Que les biens à vendre sont libres de tout privilège immobilier spécial et de toutes hypothèques conventionnelles, judiciaires ou legales. Si des inscriptions hypothécaires se révélaient, il s'oblige à en rapporter mainlevée et certificat de radiation ses frais.

5° SUR L'ETAT LOCATIF : Que les biens à vendre seront le jour de l'entrée en jouissance :

● libres de toute location, occupation ou réquisition.

● ....

....

6° SUR L'APURATION DES CHARGES DE LA COPROPRIETE (*le cas échéant*): Qu'il s'oblige à obtenir le certificat mentionnant l'apuration des charges de copropriété (*article 20, loi du 10.7.1965*) à la date prévue pour la signature de l'acte authentique, auprès du syndic dont les coordonnées sont :

....

Fig. 9. Contract of Sale — Compromis de Vente (continued).

CONDITIONS

La présente vente est consentie et acceptée sous les conditions ordinaires et de droit que l'ACQUEREUR s'oblige à exécuter, notamment :

1° Prendre les biens vendus dans l'état où ils se trouveront le jour de l'entrée en jouissance, sans pouvoir prétendre à aucune indemnité ni réduction du prix pour mauvais état du sol ou des bâtiments, vices de construction ou défauts d'entretien, la différence de contenance, fût-elle supérieure ou inférieure à 1/20, devant faire son profit ou sa perte.

2° Souffrir les servitudes passives, apparentes ou non, continues ou discontinues, pouvant grever les biens vendus, profiter de celles actives s'il en existe.

3° Acquitter, à compter du jour de l'entrée en jouissance, les impositions, taxes et charges de toute nature auxquelles les biens sont ou seront assujettis, étant précisé que la taxe foncière sera payée par les deux parties, au prorata de leur occupation dans l'année civile de l'entrée en jouissance.

4° Faire son affaire personnelle de la continuation ou de la résiliation des polices d'assurance et abonnements divers souscrits par le VENDEUR et relatifs aux biens vendus. Dans tous les cas, maintenir ces derniers assurés à une compagnie notoirement solvable.

5° Payer tous les frais, droits et honoraires des présentes et ceux qui résulteront de l'acte authentique à intervenir, ainsi que tous ceux qui en seront la suite ou la conséquence.

TRAVAUX

Le coût des travaux relatifs aux parties communes de l'immeuble sera réparti de la façon suivante :

• Les travaux décidés jusqu'à ce jour par une assemblée des copropriétaires, qu'ils soient exécutés ou non, seront à la charge du VENDEUR qui s'y oblige.

• Les travaux qui pourraient être décidés ultérieurement seront à la charge de l'ACQUEREUR, à la condition expresse suivante : le VENDEUR devra envoyer à l'ACQUEREUR, par lettre recommandée avec avis de réception et 8 jours au moins à l'avance, les documents permettant de le représenter à chacune des réunions de copropriétaires *(convocation, ordre du jour, pouvoir non limité)*.

CONDITIONS PARTICULIERES

....

....

....

....

....

PROPRIETE ET JOUISSANCE

L'ACQUEREUR sera propriétaire desdits biens à compter du jour de la signature de l'acte authentique ci-après prévue et il en prendra la jouissance à compter du ....

Fig. 9. Contract of Sale — Compromis de Vente (continued).

PRIX

En cas de réalisation, la vente aura lieu moyennant le prix principal de . . . .
. . . .
. . . . francs, payable en totalité le jour de signature de l'acte authentique. De convetion expresse, le versement effectif de la totalité du prix et du montant des frais ainsi que la signature de l'acte authentique nécessaire pour la publication foncière, conditionneront le transfert de droit de propriété au profit de l'ACQUEREUR.

CONDITIONS SUSPENSIVES

Outre la condition suspensive d'obtention de prêts *(si l'ACQUEREUR sollicite des prêts bancaires)*, les parties soumettent formellement la réalisation de la vente aux conditions suspensive suivantes :

1° URBANISME : Que le certificat d'urbanisme ne révèle aucune servitude ou charge quelconque rendant l'immeuble impropre à sa destination normalement prévisble. A ce sujet, il est précisé que le seul alignement ne sera pas considéré comme une condition suspensive, à moins qu'il ne rende l'immeuble impropre à sa destination.

2° . . . .
. . . .
. . . .
. . . .

Si l'une des conditions suspensives n'est pas réalisée, chacune des parties reprendra sa pleine et entière liberté, sans indemnité de part et d'autre et la somme remise par l'ACQUEREUR, à titre d'acompte, lui sera immédiatement restituée, et ceci sans aucune formalité.

VERSEMENT DE L'ACQUEREUR AU COMPTE SEQUESTRE

L'ACQUEREUR verse, à l'instant, au compte de . . . .
. . . . . que les parties choisissent d'un commun accord comme séquestre de ce 1er versement la somme de . . . .
représentée par un chèque . . . .

Ce versement s'imputera sur le prix convenu de la vente, sauf application de l'une des conditions suspensives contenues dans la présente convention, auquel cas elle serait intégralement restituée à l'ACQUEREUR.

MISSION DU SEQUESTRE

Le séquestre remettra au VENDEUR dans les huit jours ouvrables, copie du reçu délivré à l'ACQUEREUR et conservera la somme qui lui est confiée avec pour mission de la ventiler, le moment venu, suivant les cas exposés à l'instant.

La remise de cette somme, à l'une ou l'autre des parties selon ces prévisions, déchargera le séquestre de sa mission, sans qu'il soit besoin de reçu ou de justificatif d'aucune sorte.

Toutefois, en cas de non réalisation pure et simple, il ne pourra remettre lesdits fonds qu'en vertu d'un accord amiable signé entre les parties ou d'une décision judiciaire.

Fig. 9. Contract of Sale — Compromis de Vente (continued).

DROIT DE PREEMPTION

Les parties reconnaissent avoir été informées que la présente vente peut être soumise à un droit de préemption, si les biens à vendre sont situés dans un secteur sauvegardé, une zone d'intervention foncière, ou tout périmètre de restauration immobilière.

En cas d'exercice du droit de préemption :

- l'ACQUEREUR reprendra sa pleine et entière liberté et récupérera immédiatement et sans aucune formalité la somme remise ce jour au sequestre.

- le PREEMPTEUR, sera subrogé dans tous les droits et obligations de l'ACQUEREUR, y compris le paiement de la commission de négociation si celle-ci est prévue à la charge de l'ACQUEREUR.

INTERDICTION PAR LE VENDEUR

Le VENDEUR s'interdit, et ceci jusqu'à la signature de l'acte authentique, d'aliéner à une autre personne que l'ACQUEREUR les biens vendus, quels que soient les avantages qu'il pourra en tirer, l'ACQUEREUR se réservant le droit de demander en justice l'annulation de tous actes faits en violation des présentes, nonobstant tous dommages et intérêts.

REALISATION

Les présentes constituent dès leur signature un accord définitif sur la chose et sur le prix, et le VENDEUR ne pourra en aucun cas se refuser à réaliser la vente en se prévalant de l'article 1590 du code civil et en offrant de restituer le double de la somme versée.

L'acte authentique sera établi par Me . . . .

notaire à . . . . tél. : . . . . clerc : . . . .

éventuellement assisté de Me . . . .

notaire à . . . . tél. : . . . . clerc : . . . .

et au plus tard le . . . . sous réserve de l'obtention par ces derniers de toutes les pièces, titres et documents nécessaires à la perfection de l'acte.

2 – Clause pénale

Dans le cas où l'une des parties viendrait à refuser de régulariser la présente vente, sauf application de la condition suspensive, elle y sera contrainte par tous les moyens et voies de droit en supportant les frais de poursuites, de justice, et tous droits et amendes, et devra, en outre, payer à l'autre partie la somme

de . . . .

. . . . à titre d'indemnité forfaitaire et de clause pénale.

Fig. 9. Contract of Sale — Compromis de Vente (continued).

3 – Négociation

Les parties reconnaissent formellement que les présentes conventions ont été rédigées et négociées par

M ....

...............................mandataire, qui les a mis en présence

avec le concours éventuel de l'agence ....

En conséquence, sa mission étant terminée par la signature du présent acte, elles lui accordent irréductiblement le montant de la rémunération prévue au mandat no. ...

....

signé en date du ....et rappelé ci-après :

— La somme de ....

.........................T.V.A. incluse, à la charge du VENDEUR.

— La somme de ....

.... T.V.A. incluse, à la charge de l'ACQUEREUR.

Cette somme d'un montant total de ....

....francs
sera prélevée sur les premiers fonds versés par l'ACQUEREUR, les parties autorisant d'ores et déjà tout tiers détenteur (sequestre, notaire, mandataire) à effectuer ce prélèvement avant toute autre affectation ou remboursement quelconque, dès levée de la dernière condition suspensive de vente.

En cas d'exercice du droit de préemption, la commission restera due selon les prévisions du mandat : le VENDEUR pour la part prévue à sa charge, le PREEMP-TEUR pour la part prévue à la charge de L'ACQUEREUR.

Si par suite d'un accord amiable les parties convenaient de résilier purement et simplement le présent acte, elles s'engagent solidairement à verser au rédacteur des présentes, à titre d'indemnité compensatrice

la somme forfaitaire de ....

.... francs.

Fig. 9. Contract of Sale — Compromis de Vente (continued).

4 – Pouvoir

Les parties donnent pouvoir et qualité au REDACTEUR des présentes pour soumettre le présent engagement à l'enregistrement en vue de lui conférer date certaine et pour le déposer aux minutes du Notaire ci-dessus désigné afin d'obtenir la réitération ou la réalisation en la forme authentique dans les conditions prévues par l'article 37 du décret du 4 janvier 1955, modifié par le decret no 59-89 du 7 janvier 1959.

Ce pouvoir ne pourra être révoqué que du consentement des deux parties et prendra fin lors de la rédaction de l'acte authentique.

5 – Attribution de juridiction

Tous litiges à survenir entre les parties seront de la compétence exclusive des tribunaux du ressort de la situation des biens à vendre.

Fait à . . . .

le . . . . en . . . . exemplaires, dont un pour l'enregistrement.

. . . . mots Les parties soussignées affirment, sous les peines édictées par l'article 8 de
. . . . lignes la loi du 18 avril 1918 (article 1837 du Code général des Impôts), que le
Rayés comme nuls présent engagement exprime l'intégralité du prix convenu.

Le vendeur (1)   *l'acquéreur (1)*

Fig. 9. Contract of Sale — Compromis de Vente (continued).

All the main conditions of sale are clearly set out in the compromis de vente. These include:

● The responsibilities of the vendor and purchaser.

● Any easements that affect the property — such as public footpaths.

● Any government pre-emptive rights — such as water testing or special regional development projects.

● The conditions suspensives.

● The agreed price and method of payment.

A deposit is paid — normally ten per cent — on the signing of the compromis de vente. This is held by a third party (the agent immobilier or the notaire) until final contracts are signed.

Properties are usually bought as seen in France because owners are bound by law to reveal all the defects they are aware of. Unfortunately this is no guarantee that all is well. In the event of a problem arising after sale the purchaser finds himself in the unenviable position of having to prove that the fault was likely to be known before the signing of the compromis de vente. For properties more than ten years old the services of a surveyor (**expert géométre**) are recommended. A full structural survey is expensive, but much cheaper than dealing with an infestation of woodworm or subsidence.

The promesse de vente

This is a shortened version of the compromis de vente. Here a time for completion is set against an agreed price and certain legal conditions and requirements.

Although the buyer has a period of 'time to reflect' he is still likely to lose his deposit if he pulls out of the deal.

The 'promesse' is really a unilateral agreement to sell, whereas the 'compromis' is binding on both parties. As the purchaser is the most likely party to go back on the agreement the 'promesse' has few advantages for him. The bilateral 'compromis' is the contract to go for.

Whichever agreement is signed, this leads to the **acte authentique** which is the final conveyance of the property from seller to buyer.

The acte authentique

The notaire will produce a draft contract (**projet de l'acte**) a week or so before the completion date. This is sent out with a letter of convocation which reminds both parties of the date agreed to meet and sign the final agreement.

The acte authentique is essentially the same contract as the compromis de vente. Additionally it will:

● Clearly identify the property and land.

● Provide an analysis of ownership rights for at least the previous 30 years. Where the property itself is new this will only refer to ownership of the land.

● Refer to searches made and certificates issued. These relate to planning regulations, easements and guarantees.

Power of attorney

French law requires both parties to be present at the signing of contracts. This could involve an English purchaser in extra journeys to France, unless he signs a **mandat** (power of attorney). This can be given to the agent immobilier or the notaire and permits him to sign the contracts on your behalf.

Legal and technical terms

Acompte	Deposit on purchase price
Acte authentique	Agreement drawn up by notaire
Acte sous seing privé	Unwitnessed private agreement
Attribution de juridiction	Formal signing of agreement
Cadastre	Town plan registry
Certificat d'urbanism	Local area search
Charges	Utility, maintenance and insurance bills
Clause penal	Penalty clause
Conditions suspensive	Special conditions in pre-sale agreement
Déclaration de sincerité	Formal acceptance of purchase price
Droit de Préemption	Mandate to make enquiries for buyer
Emoluements d'actes	Fees for the notaire's normal services
Emoluements de négociation	Fees for introducing the buyer

Engagement	Commitment (normally of vendor)
Enregistrement	Registration of title of ownership
Géométre	Surveyed accuracy of proper dimensions
Hypothèque	Property as security for mortgage
Indivision	Joint ownership
Interdiction	Ban (on the vendor assigning rights)
Jousissance	Change of ownership/new owner's rights
Mandat de recherche	Agreement with agent to find property
Marchand de biens	Real-estate agent
Moins value	Capital loss
Nue-propriété	Rights set aside during tenant's lifetime
Offre d'achat	Formal offer to buy
Paiement comptant	Paid in cash
Parties Communes	Shared parts of a property
Plan de financement	Schedule or scheme of purchase
Plus value	Capital gain
Pouvoir	Authority (of documentation)
Réalisation	To carry out or fulfil agreement
Travaux	Work (required)
Vendeur	Vendor

ADDITIONAL COSTS OF PURCHASE

There is no such thing as a typical transaction because the agent immobilier may charge either vendor or purchaser. Notaries, however, charge on a scale of fees that relate to the agreed sale price. The following list (October 1991) is fairly typical:

First £2,000 of purchase price — 5 per cent.
From £2,001 to £4,000 — 3.3 per cent.
From £4,001 to £11,000 — 1.65 per cent.
Rest of purchase price — 0.85 per cent.

(Assuming an exchange rate of 10 francs to the pound.)

There are five additional fees payable when purchasing property. These are again percentages of property price:

Taxe départementale — 4.2 per cent

Taxe communale — 1.2 per cent

Taxe régionale which varies but is typically about 1.2 per cent

Stamp duty — 0.6 per cent

Land Transfer Register (Conservateur de Hypothèques) — 0.1 per cent.

Most of these fees are similar to those payable for searchers, notices and authentications in the UK.

A sample bill

Agreed price of property	£60,000.
Sliding scale fees	
For first £2,000 (at five per cent)	£100
For next £2,000 (at 3.3 per cent)	£66
For next £7,000 (at 1.65 per cent)	£115.50
For £49,000 (0.85 per cent)	£416.50
VAT on the above (at 18.6 per cent)	£129.83
Registration fees	
Départementale (at 4.2 per cent)	£2,520
Communale (at 1.2 per cent)	£720
Régionale (at 1.2 per cent)	£720
Hypothèques (at 0.1 per cent)	£60
Stamp Duty (at 0.6 per cent)	£360
Total	£5207.83

(8.7 per cent of property price).

If five per cent (£3000) is added for agent immobilier fees the total becomes £8,207.83 — or 13.68 per cent of property price.

If the notaire also negotiates the sale (acts as agent immobilier) he almost invariably charges different rates for this service. Typically this would be:

For first £17,500 (at five per cent)	£875.00
For next £42,500 (at 2.5 per cent)	£1062.50
Promesse de vente (at 0.3 per cent)	£180.00
VAT on the above (at 18.6 per cent)	£393.85
Total	£2,511.35

The alternative grand total becomes £7,719.18 — or 12.8 per cent of property price. It is invariably cheaper to buy through a notaire.

BUYING AGRICULTURAL PROPERTY

The process of purchase is similar, but if the farm is to be worked, special conditions and benefits can apply to UK buyers:

1. The contract should include a clause that prevents a compulsory purchase order. The FNSAFER (Fédération Nationale D'Aménagement Fonciers et d'Etablisement Rural) is a national organisation that buys and develops redundant farm land. If the compromis de vente excludes this the purchaser's position is protected.

2. A government 'starter' grant is available to farmers recognised by practise or qualification who are under the age of 35.

3. Additional funding for farm modernisation is available subject to an approved **plan de dévelopment**. Again the young farmer must convince officials that he has relevant experience or qualifications. He must also prove he can keep accounts, and that farming will be his main occupation.

4. Subsidised interest rates, much resented by UK farmers, are available for many aspects of agricultural investment.

The Centre Nationale pour l'Aménagement des Structures de Exploitations has a service that checks each farmer's situation in relation to eligibility for subsidies. Their address is:

CNESEA
7 rue Ernest Renan BP 1
92132 Issy Les Moulineaux Cedex.
Tel: (1) 45.54.95.40.

Further information about prices, grants, and loans is available from:

Fédération Nationale des Experts Immobiliers
FNAIM
129 rue de Faubourg Saint Honoré
75008 Paris.
Tel: (1) 42.25.24.26.

Confédération Nationale des Experts Agricoles et Fonciers et des
Experts Forestiers
CNEAFF
6 rue St Didier
75116 Paris.
Tel: (1) 47.27.00.89.

FNSAFER is the main organisation that helps farmers with the process
of buying a farm property. They also pass on information to local SAFERS
who can provide specific information about prices and availability in their
areas. The national address is:

FNSAFER
3 rue de Turin
75008 Paris.
Tel: (1) 42.93.66.06.

7
Building or Buying a
Property under Construction

In the UK it is generally accepted that building a house — or having it built for you — is the cheapest way of buying a property. The same is almost certainly true in France.

BUILDING LAND

The French divide land into zones — **résidentiel, artisanal** and **industriel**. If land is defined on town plans as residentiel then domestic building is permitted as long as byelaws and regulations are followed.

Planning permission

Planning permission (**permis de construire**) is not, as it is in England, permission to build. The right to build is implied when you buy building land — a **terrain à bâtir**. However permission is required to erect a specific building on a specific site. If your property is a **model** (pre-determined type) from a reputable builder, then planning permission is likely to be a formality and will only take two weeks to obtain.

THE COST OF BUILDING

Most building is done through a development company. These companies invariably provide a number of 'model' properties at attractive prices. The 'models' have been carefully designed to meet with local planning regulations. Internal modifications can be negotiated subject to building regulations.

Base prices

The base price for typical models is approximately:

2 bedroom bungalow with garage, approx. 80 sq. metres	£24,000
3 bedroom bungalow with garage, approx. 120 sq. metres	£28,500
4 bedroom family house and garage, approx. 180 sq. metres	£50,000

(The above are average prices sampled from developers in eight regions in September 1991 by Macdonald Research. Prices assume 10 francs to the pound.)

Land prices

The cost of building land — the terrain de bâtir — must be added to the base price. City and suburban land can be expensive as can building plots with sea frontage. Elsewhere building land usually costs between £15 and £20 per square metre. Designated building plots are usually between 500 – 1000 square metres in coastal areas, and approximately 50 per cent bigger inland.

A 700 – 800 square metre building plot may cost around £12,000 on the cost. The same money would buy a larger plot inland.

A 700 square metre plot could be 35 metres long by 20 metres wide. A 2 bedroomed bungalow, with garage, or a 3 bedroomed bungalow without garage or a 4 bedroomed house with garage might have a floor area of 12 metres by 8 metres. These measurements would leave you with a total garden area approximately the size of a tennis court.

Supplementary costs

The following checklist provides estimates of supplementary costs:

Connections for electricity and water	£1,200
Local taxes and consents	£1,750
Notaire's fees for land purchase	£700

(Again prices are sampled and assume 10 francs to the pound.)

Total costs

A breakdown of costs for the construction of a three bedroom bungalow (120 sq. metres including garage) built on a plot of land of approximately 750 square metres would break down like this:

Construction of property	£28,500
Purchase of land	£12,000
Connection of utilities	£1,200
Local taxes and consents	£1,750
Notaire's fees	£700
Total	£44,150

For comparison purposes the national index target price for new (rural) properties of this specification is £67,200. The implication is that having a house built saves about one third of the asking price of a finished property. It is a powerful incentive.

Building 'packages' in France are fairly complete and include allowances for fitted kitchens, bathroom suites and decoration. Gardens are usually 'landscaped' as part of the deal, but this can mean little more than levelling the ground and removing rubble.

Find out exactly what you can expect for your money by asking to see recently completed examples of the builder's work. If he is not happy to oblige, look for another builder.

THE BUILDING CONTRACT

The nature of the contract is defined by French law. It will include:

● A definition of what is to be built.

● The quality standards required by the Civil Code.

● The schedule of construction and other work.

● Penalty clauses for late completion by the builder or late payment by the purchaser.

● Information about the land including assumed access rights.

● Insurance required during the construction period.

● The schedule of stage payments.

Building contracts are not standardised in the same way as those for lettings and normal house purchases.

The time between signing a contract and occupying the property is normally four to six months.

Stage payments

The building industry in France has suffered the effects of economic recession in recent years. Prices are fiercely competitive and in some cases builders have cut profit margins. This is good news for the customer, but it also reflects the vulnerability of the industry.

Standards in the construction industry are controlled and are normally high. The French do not have an equivalent expression to 'cowboy builder', which is reassuring, but some construction companies have better reputations than others. Good local research and advice can pay dividends.

Stage payments offer some protection to the customer if the builder goes bust, but if a second company is employed to complete work it will inevitably be more expensive.

The normal pattern of stage payments is:

3 per cent after planning permission and signing the contract.
10 per cent on completion of the foundations.
20 per cent on completion of the building shell.
20 per cent when water connections are complete.
15 per cent when electricity connections are complete.
15 per cent when heating and plumbing is operational.
10 per cent after landscaping work is complete.
5 per cent on completion of interior decoration.
2 per cent on the handing over of keys.

Do not part with any money until the building permit has been granted. Most developers seek permission to develop a number of plots on land they own so a permit is not usually a problem, but it is the only guarantee you have that the building is legal. If it is not, the administrative bodies can demand that you return the land to its original condition. The risk is the same if the building does not comply with the authorisation, so make sure that the house you are having built is the same as the one in the permit. Modifications require a second building permit.

French financial institutions are familiar stage payments, and loans can be phased in accordingly.

Glossary of useful words and phrases

Agrandissement	Extension
Balcon	Balcony
Bâtiment	Building
Cabinet	Small room
Cellier	Storeroom
Chambre	Bedroom
Chauffage	Heating
Cheminée	Chimney/fireplace
Construction	Construction
Couvert	Covered
Cuisine	Kitchen

Debarras	Boxroom
Environ	Approximately
Escalier	Stairway/staircase
Etage	Storey
Extérieur	Exterior
Fenêtre	Window
Finitions	Finishing
Fosse septique	Septic tank
Four	Oven
Jardin	Garden
Grenier	Attic
Living	Living room
Lotissement	Housing estate
Maison	House
Maison d'amis	Weekend/second home
Moquette	Carpet
Pavillon	Small [detached] house
Pelouse	Lawn
Pièce	Room
Plain pied	Single storey
Plafond	Ceiling
Sol	Ground
Rangements	Storage areas
Revêtement	Surface
Salle de bains	Bathroom
Salon	Sitting room
Séjour	Living room
Situé	Situated
Sous-sol	Underground/cellar
Terrain	Grounds
Terrasse	Terrace
Toilettes	Toilets
Toiture	Roof
Tout l'égout	Main drainage (system)
Viabilisé	Site with made up roads

DOING IT YOURSELF

It is theoretically possible to build your own house in France, but the sight of UK vehicles with roofracks laden with building materials is still not particularly common.

First steps

Assuming the land you wish to buy is designated as building land on the town plan, you also need to ensure:

- Suitable access is provided.

- Local byelaws are complied with.

- A building permit is required for a building that has a floor surface (**la surface hors d'oeuvre**) of more than 20 square metres and for any external modification that changes the appearance of an existing building.

- The building must meet COS (**Coefficient d'Occupation des Sols**) guidelines. This is a complex formula that relates certain kinds of building to the total constructible ground surface. In densely populated areas the coefficient may be one. This means you build on all the land available. Elsewhere the coefficient can vary between 50 and 10 per cent. At 50 per cent you need 200 square metres of land to build a 100 square metre building, at 10 per cent you will need 1000 square metres of land.

Advice is available from local mairies and the DDE (**Direction Départementale de l'Equipement**).

Supplementary costs

When land is purchased the services of a notaire are required. If a loan is needed either for the land acquisition, or for the property construction, fees will be charged for financial advice, for administration, and for registering the loan.

A survey (**géométre**) is also required. Fees for this purpose are likely to be between £300 and £500.

The compromis de vente will contain a clause that makes the new landowner fence off his boundaries. The cost of this has recently been estimated at £12 per running metre. A typical plot of about 700 square metres would cost approximately £1300 to fence.

Getting the permit

'La surface hors d'oeuvre' is defined as the total ground area of a building. For buildings of more than one storey the total of all the stories are added

together, including attics and basements. La surface also includes the
thickness of external walls, balconies and terraces. The services of an
architect (or a building company which employs an architect) are required
for any building over 170 square metres.

Whilst many houses are below 170 square metres in size this should
not be seen as a license to manage without professional backup. Only
someone with specialised knowledge will be able to draw up the required
documentation for planning approval. These include:

● A detailed site plan which includes trees, existing outbuildings,
boundaries and access.

● A scale drawing of the proposed building which includes all the
elevations.

● A rather complex form (PC 157) must be completed and returned to
the local mairie. Notification is given of the hearing at which all
aspects of the proposed construction will be discussed. The application can be rejected on either architectural or environmental
grounds.

If the proposed building is near an historical site or monument the
application is automatically referred to the department's **Architect des
Bâtiments de France**. He will make a site visit before making a ruling.

Planning permission refused

If your plans are refused you have two options:

1.   To submit modified plans, or to accept any suggested modifications.

2.   To appeal to the local Administrative Court (**le Tribunal Administratif**). This can be a long process and is not recommended.

The secret of success is to talk informally to officials at the local mairie
as you are preparing your plans. They know what is likely to be acceptable
and what will be rejected out of hand.

Plans for improvements

The 20 square metre rule applies, and formal applications are required for
projects larger than this. Any changes to an existing property must also
come within the COS guidelines.

A declaration of intent is signed (form PC 156) and sent to the mairie by registered post. This must be accompanied by:

- a site plan

- listings of specification and materials

- plans of existing structures that will be modified, or photographs with the modifications drawn in.

If there is no reply within one calendar month you can assume the application is approved.

BUYING A PROPERTY UNDER CONSTRUCTION

Despite the popular impression that UK buyers are all looking for cottages in Provence or the Dordogne, most opt to buy flats or new houses on the Channel and Atlantic coasts.

BUYING ON PLAN

Buying 'en état futur d'achèvement' is a well known purchase arrangement in France. Stage payments are similar to those for building through a developer and the law is once again on the side of the buyer. It lays down the maximum percentage payment allowed for each stage of completion, and money does not become due until architects and surveyors have issued the necessary approvals. The buyer is also protected against minor defects for two years, and against major ones for ten.

There are few bargains to be had 'buying on plan' because developments are nearly always on prime sites (often close to the sea) and they are invariably finished to high standards. Ninety per cent of such developments are apartment buildings.

In some cases the purchaser will literally see nothing more than plans and drawings. Developments are usually phased, and a second phase is likely to be an indication that the first has been successful. You should be suspicious of a development that has been completed but a number of apartments remain unsold.

Contracts are fairly standardised.

S.C.I. RESIDENCE DE LA PLAGE

CONTRAT DE RESERVATION - FICHE PARTICULIERE

Nom et Prénoms :

Adresse :   Tél. :

Profession :   Tél. :

DESIGNATION DES BIENS RESERVES

Bâtiment :   Etage :
Type :   Lot n° :   Surface :
Nombre de pièces principales : + cuisine, salle de bains, WC.
Adresse :
Cave faisant l'objet du lot n°
Garage ou parking air libre faisant l'objet du n°

PRIX FERME (sauf variation du taux de TVA)

                    Appartement   F
                    Garage ou parking
                    air libre   F

                    TOTAL   F
                            ==============

PRETS

: ORGANISME PRETEUR	:	MONTANT	:	DUREE	:
:	:	:	:
:	:	:	:
:	:	:	:

Régularisation de la vente, au plus tard dans le délai d'un mois
                         après notification du projet d'acte.

Dépôt de garantie - Montant :   Mode de paiement :

Date de livraison prévue, sauf cas de force majeure,
                         Appartement :
                         Parking :

LE REPRESENTANT DE LA S.C.I..   L'ACQUEREUR.

Fig. 10. A Contract of Reservation.

114

CONTRAT DE RESERVATION

ENTRE :

La Société Civile Immobilière Résidence de la Plage, dont le siège est à VANNES, 22, rue Lieutenant-Colonel Maury,

Ci-après dénommée "LA SOCIETE"
d'une part,

La ou les personnes désignées sur la fiche particulière en tête de la présente convention,

Ci-après dénommées "L'ACQUEREUR"
d'autre part,

Il a été convenu ce qui suit :

EXPOSE

La SOCIETE réalise sur un terrain situé à KERLEVEN, commune de la FORET FOUESNANT, cadastré E, section 45 et 46, d'une contenance de 5590 m2, transformation et extension d'un ancien hôtel et création 11 logements. Selon les termes d'un permis de construire délivré le 27 juillet 1990 par Monsieur Le Maire de LA FORET FOUESNANT sous le n°29 057 90 S0022.
La date d'achèvement concernant les locaux visés par le présent contrat, est précisée sur la fiche particulière.

L'ACQUEREUR après avoir :

1°) Pris connaissance
   a) des plans et devis descriptif de la construction ;
   b) de la note technique sommaire ci-annexée :

2°) Visité les lieux,

3°) Eté avisé que le règlement de co-propriété est en cours d'élaboration a demandé à la société d'acquérir les lots désignés sur la fiche particulière dépendant de l'ensemble immobilier susvisé, y compris les fractions indivises des parties communes dudit ensemble, étant précisé que le garage ou le parking indiqué sur ladite fiche sera affecté à l'usage de dépendance du local d'habitation occupé par l'acquéreur.

En conséquence, et à titre préliminaire à l'acquisition demandée par l'acquéreur, la société réserve à celui-ci qui l'accepte, les lots sus-désignés considérés dans leur état futur d'achèvement.

Conformément aux dispositions de la loi 89-1010 du 31 décembre 1989 le présent contrat de réservation sera adressé par lettre recommandée avec accusé de réception au réservataire.
Le réservataire aura la possibilité de se rétracter pendant un délai de sept jours à compter de la réception de cette lettre, la faculté de rétraction devant être exercée avant l'expiration de ce délai par lettre recommandée avec accusé de réception.

Fig. 10. A Contract of Reservation (Continued).

I - PRIX

Le prix de vente des locaux, ci-dessus désignés, et les
modalités de paiement de ce prix sont les suivants :

a) Détermination du prix

Le prix de vente des locaux ci-dessus désignés est de F.
toutes taxes comprises.
Il est ferme et non révisable si l'acquéreur n'a recours à
aucun prêt. Le prix est définitif (non révisable) si les
prêts visés au paragraphe II sont obtenus dans le délai
prévu.
Si lesdits prêts sont obtenus postérieurement, les
dispositions suivantes sont applicables :

- Le prix est révisé à compter du jour où commence ce
  dernier délai en fonction de la varation de l'indice
  INSEE du coût de la construction. L'indice de base est
  le dernier publié au jour des présentes ; l'indice à
  appliquer pour déterminer le prix révisé est le dernier
  publié au jour de la signature de l'acte de vente.

- En outre, chaque fraction du prix non payable au
  comptant au jour de la vente sera révisée en fonction
  des variations de l'indice ci-dessus indiqué. L'indice
  de base est le dernier publié au jour de la vente et
  l'indice à appliquer lors de l'exigibilité de chaque
  fraction est le dernier publié au jour de l'exigibilité.

b) Paiement du prix

Le prix sera payable de la façon suivante :

-   5 % à la signature du contrat de réservation.

-   30 % le jour de la conclusion de la vente   chez Maître
    QUERE à CONCARNEAU.

-   20 % au plancher haut du 1er étage,

-   15 % à la mise hors d'eau,

-   20 % aux plâtres terminés,

-   5 % aux menuiseries intérieures terminées,

-   5 % à la remise des clés.

Cet échelonnement concerne la partie neuve.

Fig. 10. A Contract of Reservation (Continued).

116

Concernant la partie ancienne, il sera versé :

- 5 % à la réservation

- 50 % à la signature notariée,

le reste sans changement.

II - PRETS SOLLICITES PAR LE RESERVATAIRE

Le réservataire déclare avoir l'intention de solliciter un ou plusieurs prêts, d'un montant total de   Francs pour le financement de l'acquisition des locaux ci-dessus désignés.

Le réservataire s'engage à déposer auprès du ou des organismes prêteurs de son choix, toutes les pièces nécessaires à l'établissement du dossier de demande de prêt, et ce, dans les quinze jours de la signature des présentes.

Si ce ou ces prêts n'ont pas été obtenus pour un fait ne dépendant pas de la volonté du Réservataire, dans le délai de trois mois, à compter de la signature du présent contrat, celui-ci sera considéré comme nul et non avenu.

Le présent contrat sera cependant maintenu au bénéfice du Réservataire pour un délai de trois mois, moyennant l'actualisation du prix prévisionnel, à compter du jour où commence ce nouveau délai, conformément au paragraphe I, ci-dessus.

III - REALISATION DE LA VENTE

La réalisation de la vente n'aura lieu qu'après la mise en place d'une des garanties d'achèvement ou de remboursement prévues par les articles 22 à 28 du décret n° 67-1166 du 22 décembre 1967 et au plus tard, dans le délai d'un an, à compter du jour de la signature du présent contrat.

Le Réservant devra notifier au Réservataire, par lettre recommandée avec accusé de réception, un mois au moins avant sa signature, le projet de l'acte notarié de vente ainsi que le règlement de co-propriété et l'état descriptif de division, en lui précisant la date à partir de laquelle pourra être signé ledit acte de vente.

Celui-ci sera reçu par le notaire du vendeur, dans le délai maximum de dix jours qui suivra cette date.

Fig. 10. A Contract of Reservation (Continued).

117

Faute par le Réservataire d'avoir signé l'acte dans le délai fixé ci-dessus, et sauf résiliation amiable, sommation sera faite au Réservataire, huit jours à l'avance, de se présenter à jour et heure fixés en l'étude du notaire ci-dessus désigné, le défaut de régularisation de l'acte rendant au Réservant sa pleine et entière liberté.

IV - **CONDITIONS DE LA VENTE**

Les locaux seront vendus dans l'état conforme aux plans et devis descriptifs de la construction, sous réserve d'une tolérance ne pouvant excéder cinq pour cent des dimensions indiquées et des aménagements de détail qu'il serait nécessaire d'apporter à la construction pour des raisons d'ordre technique ou administratif.

L'acquéreur en aura la jouissance à l'achèvement de la construction ; il acquittera, à compter du jour de la mise des locaux à sa disposition et dans les conditions prévues par le règlement de co-propriété, les fractions des charges communes afférentes aux lots vendus.

L'acquéreur supportera et acquittera tous droits et taxes, honoraires du notaire, salaires du Conservateur des Hypothèques et, d'une manière générale, tous les frais entraînés par la vente, y compris ceux du présent contrat.

De convention expresse entre les parties, la remise des clés n'interviendra qu'après paiement du solde du prix.

Une remise de clés tardive, par suite de la carence de l'acquéreur, n'aura pas pour conséquence de différer la date de la mise à disposition pour le paiement des fractions des charges communes, comme il est dit ci-dessus.

V - **CONCLUSION DE LA VENTE**

Selon les prévisions de la SOCIETE, la vente pourra être conclue, au plus tard, à la date indiquée sur la fiche particulière.

L'acquéreur sera convoqué pour signer l'acte de vente à : L'Etude de Maître QUERE, notaire à CONCARNEAU

La vente ne sera parfaite que par la signature de cet acte, à laquelle le transfert de propriété est expressément subordonné. Toutefois, la SOCIETE conserve la qualité de "MAITRE DE L'OUVRAGE" à l'égard des entrepreneurs, architecte et autres techniciens, jusqu'à l'achèvement de la construction.

Fig. 10. A Contract of Reservation (Continued).

VI - <u>DEPOT DE GARANTIE - INDEMNITE</u>

En contrepartie de la réservation, objet du présent contrat, l'acquéreur verse à : CREDIT AGRICOLE de QUIMPER à un compte spécial ouvert à son nom, la somme indiquée sur la fiche particulière qui restera indisponible, incessible et insaisissable jusqu'à la signature de l'acte de vente, conformément à l'article II de la loi 67-3 du 3 janvier 1967. Cette somme s'imputera sur le prix ci-dessus stipulé, comme il est prévu à l'échelonnement du paiement, lors de la réalisation de la vente.

Ladite somme sera restituée à L'ACQUEREUR, dans les cas prévus à l'article 35 du décret 67-1166 du 22 décembre 1967.

Elle sera versée et restera acquise à la SOCIETE, à titre d'indemnité dans tous les autres cas et notamment si :

- L'acquéreur ne dépose pas les demandes de prêts susvisées dans un délai de 15 jours ou ne fournit pas avec diligence aux établissements prêteurs, les précisions et justifications demandées par eux.

- S'il ne signe pas l'acte de vente au jour et heure qui lui auront été fixés.

Dans l'un ou l'autre cas, la SOCIETE demandera à

de lui verser cette somme et redeviendra libre de vendre les locaux ci-avant désignés, à toute personne de son choix.

VII - <u>REPRODUCTION DES ARTICLES 32 A 35 DU DECRET 67-1166 DU 22 DECEMBRE 1967</u>

Décret 67-1166 du 22 décembre 1967 portant application de la loi 67-3 du 3 janvier 1967, modifiée par la loi 67-547 du 7 juillet 1967, relative aux ventes d'immeubles à construire.

<u>Art. 32</u> : Le montant du dépôt de garantie ne peut excéder cinq pour cent du prix prévisionnel de vente, si le délai de réalisation de la vente n'excède pas un an. Ce pourcentage est limité à deux pour cent, si le délai n'excède pas deux ans. Aucun dépôt de garantie ne peut être exigé, si le délai excède deux ans.

Fig. 10. A Contract of Reservation (Continued).

119

<u>Art. 33</u> : Le dépôt de garantie est fait à un compte
spécial, ouvert au nom du réservataire, dans une banque ou
un établissement habilité à cet effet ou chez un notaire.
Les dépôts des réservataires des différents locaux composant
un même immeuble ou un même ensemble immobilier peuvent
être groupés dans un compte unique spécial comportant une
rubrique par réservataire.

<u>Art. 34</u> : Le réservant doit notifier au Réservataire le
projet d'acte de vente, un mois au moins avant la date de
signature de l'acte.

<u>Art. 35</u> : Le dépôt de garantie est restitué, sans retenue
ni pénalité au Réservataire :

- Si le contrat de vente n'est pas conclu du fait du
  vendeur, dans le délai prévu au contrat préliminaire ;

- Si le prix de vente excède de plus de cinq pour cent le
  prix prévisionnel, révisé le cas échéant, conformément
  aux dispositions du contrat préliminaire. Il en est ainsi,
  quelles que soient les autres causes de l'augmentation du
  prix, même si elles sont dues à une augmentation de la
  consistance de l'immeuble ou à une amélioration de sa
  qualité ;

- Si l'un des éléments d'équipement prévus au contrat
  préliminaire ne peut être réalisé ;

- Si le ou les prêts au contrat préliminaire ne sont pas
  obtenus ou transmis ou si leur montant est inférieur à
  dix pour cent aux prévisions dudit contrat ;

- Si l'immeuble ou la partie d'immeuble ayant fait l'objet
  du contrat présente dans sa consistance ou dans la qualité des
  ouvrages prévus, une réduction de valeur supérieure à dix
  pour cent.

Fig. 10. A Contract of Reservation (Continued).

120

Dans les cas prévus au présent article, le Réservataire
notifie sa demande de remboursement au vendeur et au dépositaire,
par lettre recommandée avec demande d'avis de réception.
Sous réserve de la justification par le déposant de son
droit à restitution, le remboursement intervient dans le
délai maximum de trois mois, à dater de cette demande.

                                        Fait à
                                        Le
                                        En trois originaux.

LE REPRESENTANT DE LA SOCIETE.   L'ACQUEREUR

Fig. 10. A Contract of Reservation (Continued).

The 'On Plan' contract

The main points of the contract are:

- The particular apartment is identified and described, and the price is fixed.

- The development schedule is explained.

- The rights and arrangements for co-propriété are set out according to the law of 1989.

- All stage payments and conditions of sale are set out.

Useful words and phrases

Acquéreur	Purchaser
Contract de reservation	Contract of reservation
Date de livraison prévue	Predicted date of completion
Dépôt de garantie	Deposit
Durée	Time period (for mortgage)
Maître de l'Ouvrage	Clerk of Works
Mode de paiement	Method of payment
Montant	Amount (of money)
Organisme prêteur	Lender
Prêts	Loans/mortgages
Prix fermé	Fixed price

Advantages of buying 'On Plan'

'On Plan' purchases are popular for a number of reasons.

New property
Buyers are getting a new property.

Values
Although 'on plan' apartments are at the pricier end of the market, the value of the finished apartment is invariably greater than the prix fermé. Stage payments allow the developer to maintain his cash flow through out the development process, rather than having to wait to sell the finished article. The purchaser in turn is rewarded for his 'act of faith' by having the price fixed up to two years ahead of completion.

Discount

If apartments are sold direct, the prix fermé can represent a five per cent discount as no estate agent is involved.

Choice

The purchaser can inspect the property at various stages of development. He can choose his own scheme of decoration, colour of bathroom suite, kitchen units and appliances, and can even select floor tiles from a pre-determined range.

Cash

Some buyers take advantage of stage payments by delaying loan applications, or by taking their time to dispose of other assets. Some hold cash reserves on deposit and arrange withdrawals in line with the payment schedule.

Late payments

Contracts rarely have severe penalty clauses for late payments. A month's 'grace' is common, followed by a penalty charge of around one per cent per month.

Completion stages

Contracts of co-ownership usually take six to eight weeks to complete and notaires have become famous for spinning things out longer than that. This means the buyer has to find only the deposit (usually five per cent), followed by the stage payments due by the date of completion.

Lenders

Banks are often less cautious about lending money 'on plan' than for other property purchases. This is because equity values are easy to determine, the developers are often large, successful (and solvent) companies, and the apartments themselves are easy to dispose of if repossession becomes necessary.

Developers can often arrange attractive mortgage terms. The developer of course earns commission and the bank increases its volume of mortgage business.

Legal costs

Legal costs may be reduced if one notaire is used by the developer and a number of co-owners. This is because research time and paperwork is reduced, and contracts can be drafted 'in blocks'.

Authorised representative

Power of Attorney (**mandat**) is often designated to third parties who will attend the acte de vente on behalf of the buyer. This power of attorney is not a short-cut but a safeguard. A professional — familiar with French language and civil law — is more likely to make sense of the procedure and to identify any last minute problems. This can also save the purchaser time and money by making an additional journey from the UK unnecessary.

Spotting the sharks

Although 'on plan' purchases are generally satisfactory some buyers have been disappointed, or worse still, ripped off.

It is not unknown for 'phantom developers' to set up a mobile office (generally during the holiday season) and to take deposits for a project they have little or no intention of completing. At best this is testing the market, and at worst it is fraud. Either way it will be difficult to get your money back.

Bona fide developers go to great lengths to market their apartments. They produce well drafted plans, glossy literature, and can generally point to a track record of success. If you are in any doubt ask around locally or check at the mairie.

When a development is not selling well the developer may sell a few apartments to a third party at a greatly reduced price. This third party (often an estate agent) will then offer the apartments at slightly below the prix fermé. The purchaser buys from the agent, who adds his fees into the sale price. Later he finds himself paying the developer — not the agent — the outstanding stage payments.

This is legal and it can prove to be a bargain. In most cases however it suggests that the developer was over optimistic in forecasting profit margins. The resale value of the apartments will reflect this.

When an agent is selling several apartments in the same development, be suspicious. It may be that he has been appointed to sell all the apartments — which happens — but it could also be an opportunist attempt to unload undesirable property.

8
Your Property as a Gîte Business

Many buyers of French property intend to let them out at certain times of the year. This can be an informal arrangement — letting to friends and family perhaps — or it can be a full blown gîte business.

The right place

If you intend to have a successful business certain locations are much better than others.

The most popular tourist areas are largely seasonal. The south coast, Provence, the Dordogne, parts of Normandy, and a dozen or more other areas can all produce good returns. The southern half of Brittany remains firmly the first choice of the UK gîte buyer. The area offers a unique combination of lower property values, good summer climate, the attractions of the Atlantic coast, and reasonable accessibility.

A practical decision

Buying a gîte is a practical rather than an emotional decision. A property that will convert into several small units has much to recommend it. There are plenty of gîtes available for large families or families sharing accommodation. There are relatively few offering good quality accommodation for four people or less. Buying a property as a gîte should have more to do with gaps in the market than your own preferences.

Practicality also dictates that you consider the following questions before turning your French property into a gîte business:

- Have you taken into account the cost of equipping the gîte with furniture and so on?

- Will it cost more to convert than you could sell it for after conversion?

- Have you taken the security of an empty property into consideration?

- Who will manage the property, clean and check it between lettings?

● Will you use the property and if so, when? If you are likely to want to use the property frequently during peak periods, then your financial equation could be very different from the average.

● Will having the property as a business affect the terms and conditions of your mortgage and insurance?

GITES AND THE LAW

The formalities of buying a gîte are the same as those for buying any other residential property. However you should inform the **notaire** of your intention. He will add the appropriate clause into the acte de vente which saves additional paperwork later on.

You should also inform the **Registre de Commerce** and the tax authorities. If you fail to do so punitive financial penalties can be applied.

Gîtes ruraux

All gîtes are registered in France according to the facilities they offer. Most are fairly basic and are counted as **gîtes ruraux** (rural accommodation). There are special tax allowances that can be claimed as long as the property is let out for a minimum of three months each year.

MARKETING YOUR PROPERTY

Marketing is something that is frequently overlooked. A successful gîte business is one that attracts business outside the high season, and one which customers will return to year after year. To achieve this a marketing strategy should be planned at least 12 months before the first letting is anticipated.

The options

The most cost effective is to market it yourself and to live close enough to the property to manage it. If this is not viable you must consider some alternatives.

Using an international agency

You can use an international agency. Commission rates are high — up to 20 per cent — but they do pay in a currency and place of your choice. One major problem with these agencies is that they offer no supplementary services. They provide property guides and process bookings. Important considerations such as inventories, maintenance, cleaning, laundry, and the general welfare of the property remain entirely your responsibility.

French agent
You can appoint a French agent. Commission rates are again high — around 15 per cent — but the agent will manage the property on your behalf. Bills, which include repairs and replacements, are usually added to the agent's commission. This can prove to be expensive.

Do it yourself
You can promote the property yourself and appoint a local manager. Your estate agent, notaire, or bank may be able to suggest someone suitable. Failing that there are a number of local agencies who specialise in this kind of business. Your nearest Syndicat d'Initiative should be able to make a recommendation.

Advertising
Most promotional budgets are around ten per cent of projected net income, and rather more than that in the first year. Do not overlook the value of free publicity. Your local Syndicat d'Initiative will list the property and respond to enquiries on your behalf. It pays dividends to keep them up to date on availability.

A number of UK publications are worth considering. *The Guardian, The Independent,* and *The Mail on Sunday* have all developed a solid reputation amongst gîte owners. *The Yorkshire Post, Evening Standard, Manchester Evening News,* and *Birmingham Post* lead the way amongst regional newspapers. *The Lady* remains the first choice magazine. It has been known to fill bookings by a card in a shop window and word of mouth, but don't rely on this.

When placing the advertisement make sure that you include as a minimum the following information:

● the exact location of the gîte

● the dates of availability

● the tariff structure: this is most frequently quoted as 'prices from. . .' with high season prices being up to double the stated amount

● the number of beds

● local facilities for sport and recreation

● a telephone contact number.

MAKING A PROFIT

For a gîte owner this is not necessarily a pre-requisite. The purpose is usually to make a fair return on your investment, and an incalculable factor in this is your own enjoyment of the property.

The tariff structure

You are obviously going to charge most in high season, but your rates should be competitive throughout the letting period. The amount you can ask depends on the property itself and its location, so comparing your gîte with similar properties is the best way to find out what the market can stand.

You must also be clear about exactly what you are offering. Household linen, insurance, and telephone charges are not normally included in self-catering tariffs. Tourist taxes and cleaning usually are. A few years ago guests were expected to pay for metered electricity. This is now usually included in the price, though supplementary charges for heating are not uncommon.

Scanning newspaper columns in early 1992 revealed that high season gîte tariffs ranged from £95 a week for basic four bed accommodation to £850 for a small château with room for 17. Most gîte owners were asking between £150 and £200 a week.

A formula for success

Every gîte business is different but there are common factors to consider in working out the potential profitability:

Income

This often worked out over a letting period of 36 weeks (anything more is a bonus) and is broken down into three twelve week blocks of high, medium and low tariffs.

Expenditure

This is calculated over the same time scale. This includes advertising, cleaning and refurbishment for the letting period, plus a portion of the annual bills. These bills include loans, insurances and local taxes.

Profit

Deducting expenditure from income gives you a pre-tax profit figure. If this is less than ten per cent of the market value of the property then the business — from a purely financial point of view — is unsuccessful. (A similar income could have been generated by investing the amount of the loan in a building society.) You can take comfort though from the fact that there are 16 weeks left to enjoy the gîte yourself.

Sample calculation

As a simple rule of thumb, if the property is let for three-quarters of the year, then three-quarters of the annual bills can be set against income.

Value of property —	£40,000
Income	
12 weeks at £160	£1,960
12 weeks at £120	£1,440
12 weeks at £100	£1,200
Total	£4,600
Expenditure	
Proportion of annual loan repayments	£2,300
Proportion of utilities and local charges	£600
Cleaning and management	£500
Advertising	£400
Repairs	£230
Replacements	£70
Total	£4,100
Pre-tax profit	£500

Not many gîte owners do as well as this, but a few do rather better. Even sustaining a loss according to this formula need not be a disaster. The property itself is an investment and there are owners who suggest that persuading others to pay part of their mortgage is success in itself. The important thing is to approach the idea of a gîte business realistically. After all, there are trouble free investments which can prove to be more profitable.

A fringe benefit of a gîte business is that the French tax authorities allow you to offset all refurbishment costs against letting income. This should mean, in the early years at least, your tax bill should be minimal.

THE GITE AS A BUSINESS

A gîte business counts as self employment in France. You are not only taxable but you will have to pay social security contributions. You must register yourself with the local Chamber of Commerce (**Chambre de Commerce**) who will require:

● a Carte de Séjour [See Chapter 4]

● an attestation from your notaire that the property is legally yours

● your passport and additional passport photographs

● your birth and marriage certificate, and possibly other family documentation.

If the Chambre de Commerce are satisfied with your bona fides you will be entered on the register as a **Louer en Meubles Professionnel** (professional renter of furnished accommodation).

You are now in the gîte business.

9
Setting Up a Business in France

THE PROFESSIONAL ADVISORS

A gîte business is an obvious choice for those choosing to maximise the profitability of their property investment.

An early point of contact for those considering setting up other kinds of company or business will be the notaire or agent immobilier. Their role is similar to that which applies to domestic property. Even if you intend to work from home you are still required to set up the business formally and to follow registration procedures.

The Notaire
The notaire again acts on behalf of all parties to a contract for the purchase of a business and commercial property. The final stage of contract — the acte de vente — is again a notarised deed which only the notaire can complete.

His fees for the purchase of an existing small business — a fonds de commerce — are normally between 16 and 18 per cent of purchase price.

The Agent Immobilier
Most business sales are handled in the early stages by an agent immobilier. He draws up preliminary contracts and can complete all formalities except for the acte de vente.

This is invariably a cheaper option. Total commission charges are likely to be between eight and ten percent of the agreed purchase price.

The Avocat or Conseil Juridique
The closest equivalent to these professionals in the UK is perhaps the specialist legal executive. Their offices are most commonly found in Paris and the larger cities.

Since 1991 the role of the avocat and conseil have been formally identical. Like the agent immobilier they can complete all formalities except for authenticating the final contract.

For the purchase of a business there are distinct advantages in using the services of an avocat.

- They are invariably specialists at setting up different kinds of companies, and often work exclusively in the commercial area.

- They can offer advice on commercial and fiscal matters.

- They will have an up to date understanding of civil and employment legislation.

- They charge at an agreed hourly rate which is often cheaper than the commission rates of agents and notaires.

WHAT KIND OF COMPANY?

French law allows a bewildering range of different kinds of companies. Each has a separate identity. The most common are:

Société à Responsabilité Limitée
Very similar to the UK limited company. Liability is limited to at least two, and no more than 50 shareholders, who are expected to have an annual general meeting. The minimum legal share capital is FF50,000. Although it may seem rather technical it is probably the best option for the husband and wife team who intend to work mainly from home.

Enterprise Unipersonnelle à Responsibilité Limitée
This is an alternative version of the limited company. It permits a single shareholder with FF50,000 share capital. This form of limited liability is a sensible option for the small trader or individual who is working from home.

Enterprise Individuelle
Similar to the UK sole trader. This is an inexpensive option to set up but liability is unlimited. It is really only suitable for a part-time or small turnover business, but it remains the most common option for those who choose to work from home.

Société Civile
This style of company requires at least two named shareholders. No shareholding capital is involved but liability is apportioned according to

the number of shares held. This format is most common when a business is based on land ownership.

Société en Commandité

An unusual hybrid company set up. It involves active and sleeping partners. Active partners are fully liable, but liability for sleeping partners is limited to the amount they have put into the business.

Société en nom Collectif

Here there are no minimum capital restrictions for at least two share-holders. These shareholders are responsible for company debts, but are treated as sole traders for tax and social security payments.

Société Anonyme (SA)

This is a common format for companies who hope to attract venture capital in return for possibly a high turnover and large profits. There are at least seven shareholders with a minimum total shareholding of FF225,000. Shares may be bought on a subscription basis over a period of five years.

Succursale

This amounts to a branch office. Formalities are limited to registering the company and its articles of incorporation. The French branch office keeps independent accounts. Trading practices, tax, and social security matters become subject to French law.

The definition of what constitutes a French branch office or agency — the Succursale — is a complex one. Essentially the French authorities will look at the way business is conducted. Key pointers include:

● Whether or not contracts, invoices, and receipts are issued locally.

● Is at least one member of the branch staff resident in France for most of the year?

● Is a local manager conducting business negotiations directly with customers?

The advantages of the branch office include:

● The cheapness and lack of formality required to establish it.

● The branch office's profits and losses can be taken into account in accounting the parent company's income.

Subsidiaire

An alternative to the branch office is the subsidiary. This is characterised by the decision making and economic control of the parent company. It is nevertheless fully registered as a French company and subject to French law and taxation.

The subsidiary is more complex and expensive to establish than the branch office. However it offers certain advantages:

● Greater management flexibility because of autonomous legal stature.

● Parent company liability is limited to a modest stake in the subsidiary's capital.

● The subsidiary can pay the parent company for financial and technical services. These costs can be deducted from taxable income.

● The subsidiary allows the parent company to cooperate with third parties in France who acquire holdings.

Bureau de Liaison

This is sometimes called a shop window. It is the legal form that allows a foreign business to communicate with potential customers — normally through advertising.

Any staff employed should not have decision making autonomy or carry out normal management operations.

SET UP COSTS AND FORMALITIES

The French government have been accused of not making it easy for foreigners to set up a business in France. Since 1st January 1992, however, the procedure has become simplified. In theory at least the UK businessman should have no more problems than his French counterpart.

Exchange controls

These were removed in January 1990. There are therefore no restrictions on the repatriation of dividends, foreign investments, or profits.

Registration

You are required to register the new business at the **Registre du Commerce** within two weeks of starting to trade. You will require:

- A company statute. This defines the business in terms of its legal structure, share capital, trading address and activity.

- Proof that share capital has been paid to a notaire or deposited in a bank.

- Documents of incorporation. These are sent to an administrative department — the **Centre de Formalités des Enterprises** — and to the commercial court (**Greffe du Tribunal du Commerce**) who in turn inform the tax and social security departments that you are in business.

- A notice of incorporation for publication in a legal register — the *Bulletin of Civil and Commercial Properties.*

- Standard form notices for local newspapers.

- An application to register with the **Répertoire des Métiers** (Trade Register), the **Chambre de Commerce et l'Industrie** (Chamber of Commerce and Industry), and possibly with local trade associations.

Professional advice

Theoretically you can deal with all these matters yourself. It is recommended though that you take professional advice. French bureaucracy is not noted for encouraging individualism. Many of these documents have to be prepared in a precise form, and will be returned if they are incomplete or imprecise.

Registration fees

There are both fixed and flexible charges. According to one trade survey the average cost of completing business set up formalities in 1992 was just over 8,500 francs.

A typical breakdown would be:

Registering a limited company	1,200 francs
Tax on authorised share capital outlay	430 francs
Incorporation fees for a limited company	3,200 francs
Legal announcements and print costs	1,100 francs
Additional professional services	2,700 francs
Total	8,630 francs

BUYING COMMERCIAL PROPERTY

Fonds de Commerce

The legal process for buying business premises is similar to that for the purchase of domestic property.

However there is one important difference. In French law the property is a separate entity to the business itself. The business — the fonds de commerce — includes the trading name, licences, vehicles, fixtures and fittings, stock, and intangible assets that includes goodwill.

The fonds de commerce is, in effect, a separate contract. The business can sometimes be sold, or reassigned, without the property itself changing hands.

The Preliminary Contract

The contract for the purchase of commercial property includes the following elements:

- Agreed price and method of payment.

- A deposit — normally ten per cent of the agreed price — which is held by the selling agent or notaire.

- The legal identification of the property itself and the vendors and purchasers.

- A description of any additional rights or restrictions that apply to the property.

- The vendor's declaration that the property is sold with vacant possession.

- An agreed date for completion.

- Any special conditions (**clauses suspensives**) that will terminate the transaction. One such condition may be that the deal is subject to the buyer raising a loan or mortgage. As with domestic property this protects the deposit if the deal cannot be financed.

LEASING COMMERCIAL PROPERTY

Almost half of the commercial property in France is leased. Leases are for a minimum of nine years unless a shorter period is agreed in advance by both parties.

As with domestic property the commercial lease is weighed heavily in favour of the tenant, and formally the documents are very similar.

Renewing the lease

Although the business is legally separate from the building, it is recognised that in practise the two are interdependent. The tenant therefore has the right to renew the lease by informing the landlord of his intention to continue trading. This must be done, in writing, six months before the lease expires.

Rent

This is negotiable and becomes part of the formal agreement. Sometimes the amount payable is linked to an agreed index, with the provision that any rise or fall of more than 25 per cent will be subject to an independent review. This would take into account market trends, property values, and base rates.

If the rent is not indexed the landlord is allowed to change (which invariably means increase) the rent every three years. These increases may not be more than the standard index of the cost of housing construction during the three year period. The only exception to this is if the premises have been improved at the landlord's expense, and this must add more than ten per cent to the property's market value. Even in these circumstances the law provides strict limits on how much more the landlord can charge.

Hotels and certain kinds of office properties are subject to slightly different rules. In some cases rent increases may be related to business turnover. This is similar to the situation in which the tenant of a UK public house can find himself. Successful trading sometimes appears to be 'punished' by a substantial rent increase. In France though increases have to be rather more justified than arbitrary.

The responsibilities of the tenant

Again these are very similar to those applied to a domestic lease. Basically the tenant is responsible for regular payment of rent and the other charges on the property.

Contact clauses may limit the kind of business activity he may carry out from a particular property. The landlord's approval must also be sought for a change of trading activity, or any sub-letting of the property.

The landlord can also insist that any activity is formally registered with the appropriate trades organisation and subject to their rules. These restrictions are necessary because tenants of commercial property often transfer responsibility for the lease from themselves to their business. This, in turn, could be either sold or reassigned.

Droit au bail

A deposit — the **droit au bail** — is required at the time the lease is signed. This is normally the equivalent of three or six months' advance rental. The amount is normally returnable at the end of the lease period.

Eviction compensation

If the tenant has fulfilled his obligations, and the renewal of a lease is refused, he is entitled to compensation.

Again there is a complex formula which takes into account the value of the business, the cost of relocation and re-settling, and any additional staff travel costs.

In practice eviction compensation is not something that many landlords would contemplate. They are more likely to find a pretext — such as a change in trading activity made without the landlord's approval.

FINANCING A BUSINESS

The business plan

French banks may be approached with a business plan. This should be prepared to a professional standard and drafted in French. It will include:

- a market evaluation

- a full description of the intended operation

- details of intended capital purchases, including property and leases

- the intended legal format and constitution of the company

- cash flow forecasts

- a full asset and investment profile

- a forecast of accounts for the first three years of trading.

For anything more than the most modest business venture, this information should be compiled by an accountant (**un comptable**) or a professional auditor (**Commissaire au Comptes**).

Business loans

Finance is generally raised from one of three sources:

A UK bank

A UK bank will approach the matter in much the same way as it would for the setting up of a UK business, but is likely to require additional security and safeguards.

The venture capital sector

One way in which French companies raise money is through the circulation of a promotional prospectus on the capital markets. This accounts for around 40 per cent of credit and short term finance. Rates of interest are very competitive.

A French Bank

French banks offer a number of arrangements. The principal forms of finance generally amount to loans or leasing contracts for between two and 20 years. Loans are normally available for up to 80 per cent of the total investment subject to depreciation of stock and equipment.

When the business involves a property purchase, even where this is domestic premises used as a small business base, the loan will invariably be secured against the property.

100 per cent finance is sometimes available for certain leasing arrangements. In this case a leasing company owns the premises for the duration of the lease, but the tenant has the right to buy when the lease contract is terminated.

French banks will normally require the following guarantees:

- a charge on the business

- a mortgage on the property

- a charge on certain items of equipment

- an inventory of possessions

- insurance cover assigned to the bank.

Cheaper loans

Loans for smaller amounts,which must also not add up to more than 50 per cent of the business, can sometimes be obtained on preferential rates from trade organisations.

Another form of loan is possible if you join a franchise network. In this case a bank will accept guarantees from a mutual guarantee society set up on behalf of the franchise operators. In some cases it is possible to obtain a loan that included the cost of joining the network.

Traditionally interest rates in France have been lower than in the UK. This was however dramatically reversed at the end of 1992.

Tax breaks and incentives

The French government is keen to encourage employment and to support investment in the country. This means:

● Government subsidised loans are available to certain kinds of craftsmen and traders.

● Industrial businesses grants and subsidies are available on a regional basis. This is similar to the regional aid programme operating in the UK. It is EC funded and intended to help commercial and industrial regeneration. Information is available from the Conseil Régional in each area.

● Indirect grant aid is available in the form of tax abatement for new businesses. 100 per cent abatement on profit taxation applies for the first two years. This is followed by a sliding scale that reduces to a 25 per cent abatement in the fifth year. Independent professionals, and those selling financial services and insurance do not enjoy this abatement.

● Taxes professionnelles are not levied in the first year. These are similar to the old UK rates system. The charge is based on a notional rental value of the property and assets. The bill can vary considerably according to location, and exemptions beyond the first year are also determined on a local basis.

● Up to 25 per cent of the initial investment in a business can be offset against personal income tax. The ceiling here is FF 10,000 for a single person and FF 20,000 for a married couple.

EMPLOYING OTHERS

Permits required

Traditionally all those who work in France require a work permit (**carte de travail**) and residence permit (**carte de séjour**).

This now only applies to non EC personnel. Members of the EC are now given renewable five year residence permits, but these still require full documentation.

Working hours

This has been defined since 1982 as:

- A standard 39 hour working week. Overtime is non-mandatory and must be paid at enhanced rates.

- Employees cannot be required to work on Sundays.

- A minimum paid holiday allowance of five weeks plus the 11 national holidays.

- Part-time contracts are notionally pro-rated. In practice this is difficult to administer and enforce. Most French people take their holidays in August, and most businesses are also closed on bank holidays. For all practical purposes most activity grinds to a halt for seven weeks each year.

Minimum wages

France has minimum wage legislation. However this has been largely unenforceable since France began to suffer a significant unemployment problem in recent years.

Theoretically the legal minimum wage is linked to the cost of living index.

In September 1992 the legal minimum was FF 31.91 as an hourly rate, or 5,554.79 for a standard 169 hour month.

Semi-skilled workers normally receive a minimum wage 15 to 20 per cent higher than the legal minimum. Skilled workers receive 40 to 50 per cent more. Management salaries are mostly within the range of FF 12,000 to 40,000 per month.

Special conditions apply to those working in the hotel and catering sectors.

Contracts of employment

Anyone employed in France is entitled to a written contract. This covers three main areas:

- the job description

- the wage agreed

- the legal position of the employee in terms of responsibilities within the company.

The contract can be for a fixed or indefinite period. Any contract that does not state the fixed period of employment is deemed to be indefinite.

Stringent warnings and procedures have to be followed before an employee can be dismissed from an indefinite contract. This is intended to prevent arbitrary dismissals. The only genuine reasons accepted are proven criminality, misconduct or professional inadequacy.

Disputed cases are judged by a tribunal. Wrongful dismissal invariably brings a substantial entitlement to compensation. The terms of this **Indemnité de Licenciment** are fixed by a special legal formula.

Fixed contracts must not be for longer than two years. Unless the employer can prove just cause for an earlier termination, the employee will receive a compensation sum at least equal to the remaining portion of his contract.

Welfare payments

Foreign companies with a base in France have to contribute to employment, health and retirement schemes on behalf of their employees. Those in employment also make their own contributions. The only exception to this is in the case of temporary employment from other EC countries.

Contributions by, and on behalf, of part-time workers are pro-rated according to the hours actually worked. In practice this is usually worked out as a proportion of income during a 'standard' month. Contributions to the French welfare system have been traditionally higher than in the UK. In July 1992 the principal elements were:

	Contribution Percentage		**Earnings Ceiling**
	Employer	*Employee*	
Sickness, maternity and disability	12.6%	5.9%	Full amount

State pension	8.2%	7.6%	Up to FF 141,732 per annum salary/wage
Widow's insurance	Nil	0.1%	Full amount
Family allowance	7.0%	Nil	Full amount

COMMUNICATIONS

On line services such as telephone, fax, and modem links are readily available and promptly installed.

Transmission

French communication systems tend to be as technically advanced as those in the UK, yet the failure rate is rather higher. Mobile phones, for instance, are still regarded as a source of much frustration. Engineering advances have however cleared a number of blackspots.

The problem is that the demand has constantly exceeded the number of lines and channels available. During the CB boom of the 1970s, for instance, it became virtually impossible in some areas for the police to use their own frequencies.

Computers

Computers are engineered to international standards, but configured for country of sale. French keyboards do not use the familiar Qwerty format. Software is written to take account of this in both XT and AT formats. Printers are configured slightly differently — to accept, for instance, the ff sign rather than the £.

A UK standard television cannot be used as a VDU. The PAL and SeCAM systems are incompatible. This will not affect PC users, but means that popular games consoles may not function without a compatible monitor.

Fax and modem

These will operate exactly the same way as in the UK, other than the fact that the Mercury option is not available.

SETTING UP BUSINESS AT HOME

Domestic and commercial property

The situation is very similar to that found in the UK. Often it is a fine line that distinguishes domestic from business premises, but the judgements are usually based on the property itself and whère it is situated.

A general rule is that each building is liable for rates either as domestic or commercial premises. The fact that your home may also be your registered office does not mean that the premises themselves are commercial. That is determined by the scale and type of activity carried on there.

In certain circumstances part of a domestic property could become liable for **taxes professionnelles** — business rates. This would apply typically perhaps to a doctor or architect when part of his domestic premises are set aside and equipped exclusively for business use. Where this happens the property is divided for tax purposes into domestic and commercial sectors.

Another complexity arises from the fact that if you have a business in France you must also have a registered office. This, however, is not necessarily either your home or business premises. For the first two years, for instance, you can legally register your business at the office of your notaire.

Business and domestic loans
As in the UK there are loans for different purposes. A self-employed writer, artist or craftsman working from home would apply for a domestic mortgage. The bank would understand that the nature of this profession meant that an area may be set aside as an office or studio.

Future development
This has been described as 'a canvas of grey areas'. Adding an extra room, for instance, would probably not affect the tax, rates, or loan situation. The assumption would be that the property was still primarily residential. Plans to build a studio that is wholly separated from the house could be interpreted differently.

The local town hall and chamber of commerce can advise in each case. Your business will already be registered with them and it is usually possible to get a quick ruling.

Other checks and safeguards
If you intend to work from home you should also make sure:

● That you have obtained you **carte de résident** (residence card) from the local Préfecture de Police.

● That your notaire is informed at the time of the property purchase that you intend to run a business from home. This will ensure that the terms of your freehold or lease do not exclude business activities. This is rarely a problem — unless the property is held under one of the many French formats of co-ownership.

● That your type of business can legally be run from home. Local trade associations and the Chamber of Commerce can offer advice here. In the larger cities byelaws forbid particular forms of business on domestic premises. Generally however the French tradition of personal liberty is upheld, but you would be unwise to think this extended to noisy nightshifts in a workshop in the middle of a housing estate.

● That your insurance cover is extended to business usage, and in certain cases, public liability.

Additional legal and technical terms

Acte de commerce	Business or commercial activity
Action (une)	Share
Actionnaire	Shareholder
Amortissement	Depreciation
Associé	Partner
Augmentation de capital	Capital increase
Bail commercial	Business or commercial property lease
Bénéfice (un)	Profit
Capitaux permanents	Long term resources
Carte de Commerçant	Trader's permit
Chiffre d'affaires (un)	Turnover
Commercial	Commercial district or property
Commerçant	Trader
Compte séquestre	Deposits held in a special account
Commissaire au comptes	Auditor
Comptable (un)	Accountant
Conseil juridique	Professional legal advisor
Constituer une société	Form a company
Entreprise (une)	A company, business, or firm
Entreprise individuelle	One man company
Faillité (la)	Bankruptcy
Fonds de commerce	The business, trade name, goodwill etc
Hypothèque	Mortgage
Immobiliations	Fixed assets

Indemnité d'éviction	Eviction compensation
L'apport initial	Opening capital
Liquider une société	Wind up a company
Materiel professionnel	Office supplies and equipment
Passif (un)	Depreciation
Registre de Commerce	Companies Register
Répertoire des Métiers	Trades Register
Taxes professionelles	Taxes on profits
Valeur nette comptable	Net book value
Valeur vénale	Market value

10
Business Taxation and Insurance in France

THE AUDIT

With very few exceptions businesses registered on French soil must present an annual audited statement to the local Commercial Court.

Requirements for audit

A detailed balance sheet
This lists fixed assets, current assets, and pre-paid expenses. Loss provision, accounts due, accrued expenses and deferred credits appear on the debit side.

A statement of income
This details expenses and revenues that come from trading and financial transactions.

An auditor's statement
This includes familiar phrases about 'the true and fair view' of the business's financial situation.

All registered companies are required by law to appoint an approved statutory auditor. He has to be independent of the client company and may not be involved in preparing the financial statements on which he reports. Auditors are normally appointed for a six year term. The following organisation can offer help with detailed enquiries:

Société Accredité de Représentation Française
2 Rue des Petits Pères
75002 Paris.

INITIAL TAX LIABILITY

Initial tax liability depends on whether you are starting a new business or taking over an existing one.

Starting a new business normally involves the purchase of a fonds de commerce. The transfer duties apply to all assets transferred apart from goods subject to VAT (TVA).

The existing scale of charges is:

Property Value Tax	National	Département	Local	Total
Less than 100,000 ff	Nil	Nil	Nil	Nil
From 100,001 ff to 300,000 ff	6%	0.6%	0.4%	7%
Value in excess of 300,001 ff	11.8%	1.4%	1%	14.2%

Transfer Duty (Droits d'enregistrement)

In the case of a business takeover there is a one off transfer duty charge of 4.8%. If however the new company is formed as a Société Anonyme (one form of limited company) there is no duty payable — as long as the legal transfer took place outside France.

Capital Gains Tax is not applied to business purchases.

BUSINESS LICENCE TAX (TAXE PROFESSIONNELLE)

In many ways this is similar to the business rate system formerly applied in the UK. It is based on an agreed rental value of fixed assets. This includes a notional market value of a rented property. A distinctly French feature of the tax is that the fixed assets figure is taken to include 18 per cent of salaries paid in the tax year before last. The tax is abated in the first year, then generally on a sliding scale for up to five years.

The amount levied can vary enormously in percentage terms according to the local incentives given to attract business. To complicate matters further, taxe professionnelle is a political hot potato. The policy, and therefore the amount charged, can change considerably following each round of local government elections.

In 1992 the lowest rate of taxe professionnelle levied in France was 11 per cent. The highest was 26 per cent and the median national average was 17.14 per cent.

A typical small business bill may work out like this:

	FF
Value of property	670,000
Value of additional fixed assets	170,000
18% of payroll	80,000
Total charge value	920,000
Total tax payable at National Median Rate	157,688

CAPITAL GAINS TAX (TAXE SUR LES PLUS VALUES)

This is divided into short and long term gains. Short term is defined as gains on assets held for less than two years. It also includes a portion of the revaluation of depreciable fixed assets held for less than two years. Long term gains are the sale of assets held for more than two years. The rates applied are:

● short term gains — 39 per cent

● long term gains — 25 per cent for land assets and 19 per cent for fixed assets. If a company is subject to Corporation Tax this last figure is reduced to 16 per cent.

CORPORATION TAX

All business registered in France is subject to Corporation Tax (**Impôts sur les Sociétés**) apart from:

● new businesses which are exempt for three years

● certain small businesses eligible for taxation under the simplified Business Income scheme.

The tax is currently 42 per cent of distributed profits, and 39 per cent of undistributed profits. It is collected quarterly.

The definition of taxable profit is similar to the formula applied in the UK. The main elements are:

- The difference between the cost value of stock at the beginning and end of the year. Added to this is the value of services, subsidies, and income from fringe profits such as interest payments.

- Allowance expenses to set against this include the cost of salaries, welfare payments, interest on loans, depreciation of equipment, education and training expenses, and the purchase of certain goods.

TAXATION OF BUSINESS INCOME

This is the small business alternative to Corporation Tax, and is known as the **Impôt sur les Bénéfices Industrielles et Commerciaux**. The definition of a small business can be complex, but it is normally taken to include:

- sole traders

- a partnership based on a limited liability company

- a family owned limited liability company.

Businesses that qualify have profits taxed on a basis very similar to personal income tax, although taxable profits are calculated as for Corporation Tax.

The Taxation of Business Income scheme has advantages when the chargeable rate of Income Tax is lower than Corporation Tax. This applies to most small businesses. In exceptional circumstances however it may be advantageous to change the legal identity of the business in order to fall into the net of Corporation Tax.

WAGES TAX

Wages tax (**Taxes sur les salaires**) is regarded as a claw-back tax — rather similar to Class 4 National Insurance in the UK. It is applied only to businesses not required to register for VAT. In 1992 the following rates were applied:

Company wage bill (FF)			Percentage charge
Nil	–	37620	4.25
37621	–	72662	8.50
72663	–	Upwards	9.50

VALUE ADDED TAX

All business operations in France are theoretically liable for VAT (**Taxe sur la Valeur Ajoutée**) as long as an 'economic activity' is involved. This of course creates a number of grey areas. A **bureau de liaison** ('shop window') does not always have to register. A branch or subsidiary office invariably does.

The French system is similar to the one applied in the UK. However there are no thresholds for registration. The requirement to register depends on the nature of business activity involved:

● Those involved in agricultural, trading, manufacturing, and service industries are required to register.

● Salaried activities are normally exempt, so are insurance and medical activities, educational services, and transactions subject to other taxes.

● Special rules apply to advertising, staffing agencies, research, and the hire of equipment and machinery.

VAT is assessed on value added at each stage of production. A credit system is applied through which VAT is charged down the chain of production to point of sale. At this stage the bill is finally paid by the customer.

The assessment applies to all amounts received by sellers and suppliers in exchange for the services received or goods sold. In the case of product, liability is incurred at the time the goods are delivered. Services can be paid on an accruals basis.

VAT payable is calculated by deducting input from output VAT. Any excess paid will be refunded.

Form CA3
The standard VAT form (CA3) must be completed quarterly by small businesses. These are defined as companies that do not pay Capital Gains Tax. Other businesses must make a monthly return.

VAT rates
The rates in force in July 1992 were:

Food, pharmaceuticals and water	5.5%
Cars, furs, perfumes and various luxury items	22.0%
Standard rate for most other items	18.6%

Imported goods are subject to VAT in accordance with these rates.

BRANCH PROFITS TAX

The general rule is that all businesses conducted on French soil are taxed as French companies. In certain circumstances however the branch may qualify to pay an additional Branch Profits Tax. In practice reciprocal tax treaties mean that this can generally be avoided.

SUPPLEMENTARY FLAT RATE TAXATION

There are three minor areas of taxation applied to certain businesses with ten or more employees. In each case the tax is levied as a percentàge of the wage bill.

Construction tax (**Participation Construction**)	0.65%
Training tax (**Participation Formation Continué**)	1.20%
Apprentice tax (Taxe Apprentissage)	0.60%

Car tax

Tax on company vehicle ownership is levied in a similar way to the car tax imposed on individuals. The amount payable depends on the horse power of the vehicle. The rate varies between FF 5,880 and FF 12,900.

Ile de France

An additional annual levy is charged on the prime commercial sites on the Ile de France. This varies between FF 18 and FF 60 per square metre of surface area.

BUSINESS INSURANCE

Premium taxes

Insurance premiums are subject to tax at the following rates:

Motor vehicles	34.9%
Fire and combined policies	7% to 30%
Health policies	9%

Premium costs
These have been traditionally comparable with the UK. Also comparable is the way that premiums in certain areas, and for certain risks, have rocketed in recent years.

Documentation format
All French insurance policies follow a format prescribed by law:

● The risks and exclusions must be fully described.

● The level of cover and the obligations of both insurer and insured must be identified.

● The schedule describes matters that relate to the issue of the policy. These include registered addresses, the premium paid, and renewal dates.

Renewals
French policies are automatically renewed unless written notice is given at least two months before the renewal date.

Claims
All claims must be notified within five working days of the insurable event. This is reduced to 24 hours in the case of theft.

Business cover
All registered businesses are expected to have the following insurance cover:

● Motor insurances for vehicles owned by the company.

● Health insurance — the **assurance complémentaire maladie** — which is a 'top up' policy to ensure the availability of health service facilities for all employees.

● Business property insurance against fire, theft, storm and water damage, and the breakage of glass.

Additional cover
Standard business cover is regarded as a legal minimum. Many companies also pay premiums for:

- pensions and savings schemes

- accident and death cover

- consequential loss following fire, flood, or other 'natural' events

- cover for legal liabilities as the owner or tenant of a building

- transport of goods.

Job related cover

Certain types of enterprises require additional insurance cover. Architects, lawyers, and doctors require professional indemnity insurance. Cafés, hotels, restaurants and garages require public liability insurance.

The list is almost endless, and this fact alone begins to explain why the French insurance market is the fifth largest in the world.

Additional technical terms

Administration Fiscale	The tax authorities
Année fiscale (une)	Tax year
Avoir fiscal (un)	Tax credit
Déclaration d'impôts (une)	Tax return
Déduction fiscale (une)	Tax allowance
Hors taxes	Excluding taxes
Impôt retenu à la source	Withholding tax
Toutes taxes	Including taxes

Useful Addresses

AA St John Alert, Fanum House, Basingstoke, Hants RG21 2BR.

Access Headquarters, Southend. Lost Card Service tel: (0702) then 362 988 for Lloyds Bank, 352 244 for Midland Bank, 352 255 for National Westminster Bank.

Alliance Française, 101 boulevard Raspail, 75006 Paris. Tel: (1) 45.44.38.28.

Automobile Club d'Ile de France, 8 place de la Concorde, 75008 Paris. Tel: (1) 42.66.43.00.

Banque Transatlantique, 103 Mount St, London W1Y 5HE. Tel: (071) 493 6717.

Barclaycard Headquarters, Northampton. Lost Card Service tel: (0604) 230 230.

Blakes Villas, Blakes International Travel Ltd, Wroxham, Norwich, Norfolk NR12 8DH. Tel: (0603) 784141.

British Council, 9 rue de Constantine, 75007 Paris. Tel: (1) 42.89.11.11.

British Embassy, 35 rue de Faubourg St Honoré, 75008 Paris. Tel: (1) 42.66.91.42.

Centre de Impôts des Non-Résidents, 9 rue d'Uzes, 75084 Paris.

Centre National de Documentation sur l'Enseignement Privé, 20 rue Faubert, 75007 Paris. Tel: (1) 47.05.32.68.

CIC Group, 74 London Wall, London EC2M 5NE. Tel: (071) 638 5700.

CNESEA, 7 rue Ernest Renan BP1, 92132 Issy les Moulinex Cedex. Tel: (1) 45.54.95.40.

Country Holidays in France, Spring Mill, Earby, Colne, Lancashire BB8 6RN. Tel: (0182) 445511.

Crabb & Templeton Associates Ltd, Chapel Plaister, nr Corsham, Wiltshire SN14 9HZ. Tel: (0225) 810531. For advice on French commercial property and finance.

Crédit Agricole, 23 Sheen Rd, Richmond, Surrey TW9 1BN. Tel: (081) 332 0130.

Crédit du Nord, 66 Mark Lane, London EC3R 7HS. Tel: (071) 488 0872.

Crédit Lyonnais, 84-95 Queen Victoria Street, London EC4P 4LX. Tel: (071) 634 8000.

DATAR, 21-24 Grosvenor Place, London SW1X 7HU. Tel: (071) 235 5140.

FNAIM, 129 rue de Faubourg St Honoré, 75008 Paris. Tel: (1) 42.25.24.26.

FNSAFER, 3 rue de Turin, 75008 Paris. Tel: (1) 42.93.66.06.

French Consulate Edinburgh, 11 Randolph Crescent, Edinburgh EH3 7TT. Tel: (031) 225 7954.

French Consulate Jersey, La Mothe St, St Helier, Jersey. Tel: (0534) 26256.

French Consulate Liverpool, Pier Head, Liverpool L3 1ET. Tel: (051) 236 1156.

French Consulate London, 21 Cromwell Road, London SW7. Tel: (071) 581 5292.

French Embassy Cultural Section, 22 Wilton Crescent, London SW1X 8SB. Tel: (071) 235 8080.

IAMIT, 17 Gotthardstrasse, 6300, Zug, Switzerland.

International Relations Unit, Department of Health, Room 318, Hannibal House, Elephant and Castle, London SE1 6TE.

Ministry of Agriculture, Animal Health Division, Export Section, Hook Rise, Tolworth, Surbiton, Surrey.

Service d'Information des Familles, 277 rue St Jacques, 75005 Paris. Tel: (1) 43.29.12.77.

Service National d'Accueil aux Etudiants Etrangers, 69 quai D'Orsay, 75007 Paris.

The Complete France, Allez France, 27 West Street, Storrington, West Sussex RH20 4DZ. Tel: (0903) 742345.

Touring Club de France, 14 avenue de la Grande Armée, 75017 Paris. Tel: (1) 43.80.68.58.

Vacances en Campagne, Bignor, Pulborough, West Sussex RH20 1QD. Tel: (07987) 433.

Further Reading

BOOKS

Business Guide to France: World of Information (Longman, 1988). 61pp, paperback.

Cabanne, Pierre. *France*, translated from the French (Helm, 1988). 416pp, illustrated with maps.

De Monza, Jean Pierre. *Guide SVP de vos Interests*, in French (De Monza, 1991). 476pp, illustrated paperback.

Du Fufournier, Bertrand. *Buying Residential Property in France* (Chambre de Commerce Française de Grande Bretagne). 80pp paperback.

Du Sordet, Emile. *Résidences pour les Vacances*, in French (Harrana, 1991). 276pp, illustrated paperback.

Dupain, Danielle. *A Votre Service*, in French (Foulinard, 1991). 426pp, illustrated paperback.

Dyson, Harry. *French Real Property and Succession Law* (Hale, 1988). 240pp, paperback.

Golding, Jonathan, *Working Abroad: Essential Financial Planning for Expatriates and their Employers* (International Venture Handbooks, Plymbridge Distributors, 1993).

French Country Welcome (Fédération Nationale des Gîtes Ruraux/ Fivedit, 1990). 456pp, paperback.

Hamilton, Ronald. *Holiday History of France* (Hogarth Press, 1985). 256pp, paperback.

Hempshell, Mark. *How to Get a Job in France* (How To Books, 1993). 160pp, paperback.

Holland, Philip. *Living in France* (Robert Hale, 1989). 4th edition. 240pp, hardback with black and white photographs.

Jones, Roger. *How to Retire Abroad* (How To Books, 1993). 176pp, paperback.

Logan, Marie Prevost. *How to Live & Work in France* (How To Books, 2nd edition 1993).

Mazzawi, Rosalind. *Long Stays in France* (David & Charles, 1990). 261pp, hardback.

Menard, Jaques. *Co-propriété*. In French (Lefevre, 1990). 189pp, paperback.

Parkinson, Charles. *Taxation in France* (Parkinson Publishing, PO Box 294, St Peter Port, Guernsey, CI).

Scholey, Andrew. *French Homes for the British* (Wisefile, 1990). 162pp, illustrated paperback.

Thomas, Bill. *The Legal Beagle Goes to France* (Quiller Press, 1989). 154pp, illustrated paperback.

Warren, Laetitia de and Nollet, Catherine. *Setting Up in France* (Merehurst, 1989). 193pp, illustrated.

PERIODICALS

France (quarterly), Beautiful Magazines, Dorma House, The Square, Stow on the Wold, Glos. Tel: (0451) 31398.

French Property Buyer, Southbank House, Black Prince Road, London SE1 7SJ. Tel: (071) 793 0700.

French Property News, Wisefile Ltd, 2a Lambton Road, London SW20 0LR. Tel: (081) 944 5500. Fax: (081) 944 5293.

Le Magazine, Le Magazine Ltd, 74 Elms Crescent, London SW4 8QX. Tel: (071) 622 3975. Fax: (071) 978 2383. Contains a large amount of French property advertisements, lifestyle and other information.

Living France, 9 High Street South, Olney, Bucks MK46 6AA.

Overseas Jobs Express, PO Box 22, Brighton, East Sussex BN1 6HX. Tel: (0273) 440220/440540. Fortnightly newspaper featuring job vacancies.

Resident Abroad, Financial Times Publishing, 102 Clerkenwell Road, London EC1. Tel: (071) 251 9321. Glossy magazine of interest to expatriates.

Index